Focus on Phonics-2b

by Gail V. Rice

Consonant Blends

Teacher's Edition

Correlated to
The Laubach Way to Reading Series

ISBN 0-88336-450-6

New Readers Press
Publishing Division of Laubach Literacy International
Box 131, Syracuse, New York 13210

Designed by Kay Koschnick and Ann Tussing
Illustrated by Caris Lester and Chris Steenwerth

Printed in the United States of America

20 19 18 17 16 15 14 13 12 11
10 9 8 7 6 5 4 3 2

To the Teacher

Focus on Phonics-2B: Consonant Blends is a part of a series of phonics workbooks which can accompany skill books in the Laubach Way to Reading series, a basic reading and writing program. Both series are designed for adults and older teenagers.

Purpose

This workbook reinforces the sound-symbol relationships involving short vowels and consonants and helps the student to sound out new words and spell them. It begins with a review of the consonant digraphs *ch, sh, th,* and *wh* and then focuses on common beginning and ending blends. The *r*-controlled vowels *er, ir, ur, ar,* and *or* are then covered extensively, both with and without another consonant following them.

Useful for which students?

Focus on Phonics-2B: Consonant Blends is useful for students who need additional practice with consonant blends and the *r*-controlled vowels for reading or spelling.

Students using the Laubach Way to Reading series may begin this workbook any time after they have finished *Skill Book 2* and its correlated reader *City Living*. Since this workbook is limited to short vowels and *r*-controlled vowels, a student may complete it before he begins *Skill Book 3*, which covers long vowels.

Remedial students and students who are using other series to learn to read should have a fairly good grasp of the sound-symbol relationships involving short vowels and individual consonants before they begin this workbook. *Focus on Phonics-2A: Short Vowel Sounds* is excellent preparation.

How to use the student workbook and teacher's edition

The teacher's edition contains replicas of the practices in the student workbook, with the answers filled in. For each different type of practice, step-by-step instructions are provided along with the first practice of that type. You do not have to follow the suggested dialog exactly, but, before doing a practice, you should become familiar with the instructions; they provide many helpful explanations and suggestions. The instructions are designed for one-to-one teaching. With a few adaptations, most of the exercises can be used in classrooms.

In the instructions, *T.* and *S.* stand for *Teacher* and *Student.* Slash marks around a letter or letters indicate the sound for which they stand. Thus, you say /a/ like the vowel sound in *pan.* When you see slash marks around a consonant blend, as /sn/ or /nd/, say the sounds rather than the letter names. Letters in italics are read by their letter names, as *a, b, c.* When words or parts of words appear with hyphens between the letters, spell them out, as in *b-a-t.*

In each practice, you should speak slowly and clearly, repeating words if necessary. Brief directions for each exercise in a practice are printed in both the student workbook and the teacher's edition. Read these directions aloud to the student. To be sure that he has understood the directions, check his work after he has done one or two items. Correct the student's work after each exercise in a practice.

Both the amount of time a student spends on the practices and the choice of which practices he is to do depend on his abilities. A student may need a great deal of work on some skills and little or none on others. A student who has trouble learning new words may need to spend several sessions on each practice; you may want to break up the practice into smaller parts for him. A student who needs only a quick review may speed through the practices and may skip some. Adapt the workbook to each student.

As a student studies a particular blend, he may think of other words with that blend that are not in the book. Why have such words been omitted? Words with long vowels or irregular spellings of consonant sounds will be covered in later workbooks in this series. This workbook includes only short vowel blend words whose meanings are commonly known, according to *The Living Word Vocabulary* by Edgar Dale and Joseph O'Rourke (Field Enterprises Educational Corp., 1976). This national vocabulary inventory gives the meanings of words and the grade levels at which they are known.

When a student has learned the words in a group of blends, you may want to refer to Appendixes B-D, which give help with adding the endings *-s, -ing, -ed, -er,* and *-y.*

Special problems

For students who have difficulty sounding out words, refer to Appendix A for suggestions. Students with dialects, foreign students, and those with speech handicaps may not give the standard pronunciation for all of the sounds. For the purposes of this workbook, it is enough if they can hear the sounds when *you* say them, can identify the sounds with their letters, and can read the words in their own pronunciation. Other students with great auditory or visual learning problems should be diagnosed and treated by specialists; they require a more specialized approach than these materials can provide.

Description of contents

The workbook begins with a review of the digraphs *ch, sh, th,* and *wh* at the beginning and end of words. Most of the other practices cover one or more beginning or ending consonant blends (or *r*-controlled vowels). These practices often contain an auditory discrimination exercise between the blend and similar consonant sounds. The student also forms new words with the blend, reads the words, spells the words, learns a few new sight words, and reads meaningful sentences with the new words. The practices can be used in a spelling program, and the student can write the sentences as well as read them.

Special exercises help the student distinguish between *r* and *l* in beginning blends and between words ending with *-ng* and *-nk.* There are frequent reviews of groups of similar blends.

At the end of the book, special practices help the student read longer words: compound words and two-syllable words, including those ending with CC-*le* (Consonant-Consonant-*le*), such as *middle* and *simple.* The book ends with a short story that uses blend words, including some longer words.

Although we recognize that there are students of both sexes, for the sake of clarity and simplicity we chose to use the pronouns *he, him,* and *his* throughout the book.

Table of Contents

Practice 1-A: Review of Beginning Digraphs *sh-* and *ch-*

Student's page 2

1

sh-

shop

she

ch-

children

chop

2 What does the word begin with?

sh ch

1. cheek	9. chief
2. chore	10. shatter
3. shoe	11. sheet
4. cheap	12. chop
5. share	13. cheer
6. shout	14. shock
7. cherry	15. ship
8. shin	16. choose

3 Write the letters and say the word.

sh	ch
sh ack	ch at
sh ed	ch eck
sh ell	ch ess
sh ip	ch ick
sh ock	ch ill
sh op	ch in
sh ot	ch ip
sh ut	ch op

4 Read the words.

shot	chill
shock	chip
shop	chick
shut	chin
shack	chat
ship	chop
shell	chess
shed	check

5 Write the word you hear.

1. chip	9. chin
2. shop	10. shack
3. check	11. chill
4. shut	12. chick
5. shell	13. shot
6. chat	14. chess
7. shock	15. ship
8. chop	16. shed

6 Read the sentences.

Review words: what, shall

1. Do not get a chill out there.
2. The children shop for a chess set.
   Dan will write a check to pay for it.
3. Shell the nuts and chop them up.
4. That family lives in a little shack.
   There is a shed in back of the shack.
5. Ed checks the deck of the ship.
6. I shipped the gift when I got the check.
7. Ann chats with a woman in the shop.
8. The hen is with her chicks.
9. What a shock! A man robbed the shop!
10. Shall I shut up the shop?
11. Ted fell and hit his chin.
12. The cup has a chip in it.
13. The hurt man is going into shock.
    Dr. King will give him a shot.

Practice 1-A: Review of Beginning Digraphs *sh-* and *ch-*

These digraph reviews are exactly that—*reviews.* They are not intended to teach S. the digraphs, only to help him review sounds and words he is familiar with already. If S. does not know these digraphs well, you might want him to go through relevant parts of *Focus on Phonics-1A: Sounds and Names of Letters.*

Before starting a practice, read any Note at the top of the practice page. A Note gives additional special directions *for that practice only.*

1

T. says: You have seen *s-h* and *c-h* before in words. In this practice, you will review words that have *s-h* or *c-h* at the beginning.
(Point to *sh.*) What sound does *s-h* make? [S: /sh/] Good.
(Point to *shop.*) What is this word? [S: shop] Good.
(Point to *she.*) And this word? [S: she] Good.
Can you hear the /sh/ sound at the beginning of those words?

Repeat the same process for *ch.* You may want to help S. pronounce the two sounds. If S. has difficulty hearing the difference between the two sounds, or if he confuses the sounds when he pronounces them, you might write out words that are the same except for the digraph, like *chip* and *ship.* Let S. see and hear the difference, and read the words. S. will get more practice discriminating between the two sounds in part 2. You might also ask S. if he can think of other words that start with *sh* and *ch.*

2

What does the word begin with?

T. says: Now I will read some words. You listen for the beginning sounds.
If the word starts with the sound /sh/, write *s-h* in the blank.
If it starts with the sound /ch/, write *c-h* in the blank.

Go over the words, reading each word at least twice, clearly and distinctly. It may help S. to repeat the words after you, but if he does, make sure he pronounces them correctly. S. should do fairly well on this practice before going on to part 3.

3

Write the letters and say the word

T. says: What does *s-h* sound like? (Point to *sh* at top of column.) [S: /sh/]
Good. Let's review some short vowel words that begin with that sound.
(Point to *ack.*) *A-c-k* sounds like /ack/. Say /ack/. [S: /ack/]
If I write *s-h* in front of /ack/ (write the letters in), I have the sounds /sh/ and /ack/. Say those sounds as I point to them.
(Point to *sh.*) [S: /sh/] (Point to *ack.*) [S: /ack/] Good.
Can you blend those sounds together into a word?
(Help S. if he has trouble.) [S: shack] Good.
Now let's go through the rest of the words.
The vowels in the words all have short vowel sounds.
You write the letters and read the word.

In parts 3 and 4, the words are grouped by both digraphs and short vowel sounds. In part 5, the digraphs and short vowel sounds are all mixed. Obviously, S. must be very familiar with consonant sounds and short vowel sounds in order to do parts 3-6.

4

Read the words

T. says: Here are the same words that you have been making, in a new order.
Read the words.

5

Write the word you hear

T. says: Now I will read each of the words for you. Write the word you hear.

6

Read the sentences

Note the place for new words and review words at the top. The only digraph review in which a *new* word is introduced is Practice 1-B. *Review* words are mostly from the lessons in *Skill Book 2* or the correlated reader *City Living* of the Laubach Way to Reading series. If S. has not had a review word before, or if he does not recognize it, tell him the word. Go over the review words *what* and *shall* before having S. read the sentences.

For more detailed instructions on carrying out parts 3, 4, 5, and 6, please turn to pages 13-14.

Practice 1-B: Review of Beginning Digraphs *th-* and *wh-*

Student's page 3

1

th-		th-		wh-	
thank	th	this	th	whistle	wh
	th ank	the	th an	when	wh en
	th ick	they	th at	where	wh ip
	th in	there	th em	what	wh ich
	th ing		th en		
	th ink		th is		
			th us		

2

Read the words.

thin	then	which
thick	them	whip
thing	thus	when
think	that	
thank	than	
	this	

3

Write the word you hear.

1. that
2. thin
3. thus
4. them
5. thing
6. whip
7. thank
8. this
9. thick
10. when
11. than
12. which
13. think
14. then

4

Read the sentences.

New word: their

Review words: where, what, happen

1. Whip this mix. Then it will get thick.
2. Where do they live? They live there.
3. Which rug shall we get?
   A thick one is better than a thin one.
4. Thanks for thinking of me.
5. When Bob is ten, then Ted will be six.
6. What is that thing in the grass?
   Is it a whip? No, I think it is a snake.
7. What happened to their son?
8. That family has no cash in the bank.
   Thus, they cannot get their car fixed.
9. I will thank them for their gifts.
10. Jan is thinner than her sister.
11. Where do you think the kids went?
12. Which car is best? Which one do you want?
13. What things will you tell them?

Practice 1-B: Review of Beginning Digraphs *th-* and *wh-*

This practice has no auditory discrimination exercise. In the instructions below, the unvoiced sound of *th,* as in *thank,* is indicated by /th/. The voiced sound of *th,* as in *this,* is indicated with underlining: /th/.

1

T. says: In this practice, you will review words that have *t-h* or *w-h* at the beginning.

(Point to *thank.*) What is this word? [S: thank] Good.
(Point to *th.*) In *thank, t-h* has the sound /th/.
Say /th/. [S: /th/] Good.
Let's look at some more words in which *t-h* has the sound /th/ at the beginning.

Go to the next column. Have the student write the letters *th* in each blank and say each word. Follow the same procedure as for part 3 of Practice 1-A.

T. says: (Point to *this.*) What is this word? [S: this] Good.
(Point to *th.)* In *this, t-h* has a different sound: /th/.
In most words, *t-h* has the sound /th/, as in *thank.*
But in some words, like *this, t-h* has the sound /th/.
Let's review some words in which *t-h* has the sound /th/.

Have the student read *the, they, there.* Then, go to the next column. Have the student write the letters *th* in each blank and say the word. Follow the same procedure as for part 3 of Practice 1-A.

T. says: (Point to *wh.*)
You know several words that start with *w-h. W-h* has the sound /wh/.
This is a lot like the *w* sound /w/, but it has more breath to it.
You let out a puff of air as you say the sound /wh/.

(Point to *whistle.*) What is this word? [S: whistle]
(Point to *when.*) And this word? [S: when]
(Point to *where.*) And this word? [S: where]
(Point to *what.* And this word? [S: what]

Can you hear the *w-h* sound /wh/ at the beginning of the word?
That *w-h* sound is a little different from the *w* sound.
(Write down the words *witch* and *which.*)
Can you hear the difference in the beginning sounds of *witch* (point to word) and *which* (point to word)?

Say the words *witch* and *which* a few times in random order, and have the student point to the word you are saying. If the student cannot hear the difference between the two sounds, do not worry about it or continue trying to emphasize the /wh/ sound.

Go to the next column. Have the student write the letters *wh* in each blank and say each word. Follow the same procedure as in Practice 1-A for this section and for the rest of the practice.

4

The new word *their* is introduced in this part. (New words are usually used at least three times in the sentences.) Explain the difference in spelling and meaning between the homonyms *their* and *there.* Use the two words in sentences.

Practice 2-A: Review of Ending Digraph *-ch*

Student's page 4

1

-ch

catch

much

2 What does the word end with?

ch sh

1. lea sh
2. lat ch
3. crut ch
4. swi sh
5. hu sh
6. mar sh
7. dit ch
8. ca sh
9. mu sh
10. bu sh
11. hat ch
12. wa sh
13. wit ch
14. poa ch
15. ma sh
16. bat ch

3 Write the letters and say the word.

ch	ch
bat ch	hit ch
cat ch	pit ch
hat ch	wit ch
lat ch	not ch
mat ch	ri ch
pat ch	whi ch
it ch	mu ch
dit ch	su ch

4 Read the words.

pitch	catch
ditch	hatch
itch	match
witch	batch
hitch	such
notch	much
latch	which
patch	rich

5 Write the word you hear.

1. match
2. rich
3. batch
4. such
5. notch
6. catch
7. ditch
8. hatch
9. which
10. itch
11. latch
12. pitch
13. much
14. hitch
15. witch
16. patch

6 Read the sentences.

Review words: curtains, dark, four, kitchen

1. I will pitch and you can catch.
2. Jack's hands are red. They itch.
3. Bill is such a good singer.
4. My kitchen is much bigger than yours.
5. If Ed wins the match, he will be rich.
6. Mom put a patch on the rip in my dress.
7. We want to catch a big batch of fish.
8. Dan is rich. He has four cars.
9. Which eggs will hatch?
10. The curtains do not match the rug.
11. Pam digs a ditch for the water.
12. The latch lifts into this notch.
13. The witch has a black cat with her.
14. John lit a match in the dark.
15. Is there a hitch on your car?
16. Which factory makes such good cars?

Practice 2-A: Review of Ending Digraph *-ch*

1

T. says: You have seen *c-h* before in words.
In this practice, you will review words that have *c-h* at the end of words.
(Point to *ch.*) What sound does *c-h* make? [S: /ch/] Good.
It makes the same sound at the end of the word as it does at the beginning of a word.
(Point to *catch.*) What is this word? [S: catch] Good.
Catch has the *c-h* sound /ch/ at the end.
Notice that there is a *t* that comes before *c-h* in the word *catch.*
(Underline *t* in *catch.*) The *t* is silent—you don't really hear it.
Most short vowel words that end with the *c-h* sound /ch/ have a *t* before the *c-h.*
(Point to *much.*) What is this word? [S: much] Good.
This word ends with *c-h,* but there is no *t* before the *c-h.*

You might ask S. if he can think of other words that end with *c-h* or *t-c-h.*

2

What does the word end with?

T. says: Now I will read some words. You listen for the ending sounds.
If the word ends with the sound /ch/, write *c-h* in the blank.
If it ends with the sound /sh/, write *s-h* in the blank.

Go over the words, reading each word at least twice, clearly and distinctly. It may help S. to repeat the words after you, but if he does, make sure he pronounces them correctly. S. should do fairly well on this practice before going on to part 3.

3

Write the letters and say the word

T. says: What does *c-h* sound like? (Point to *ch* at the top of the column.) [S: /ch/]
Good. Let's review some words that end with that sound.
(Point to *bat.*) *B-a-t* sounds like /bat/. Say /bat/. [S: /bat/]
If I write *c-h* after /bat/ (write the letters in), I have the sounds /bat/ and /ch/. Say those sounds as I point to them.
(Point to *bat.*) [S: /bat/] (Point to *ch.*) [S: /ch/] Good.
Can you blend those sounds together into a word?
(Help S. if he has trouble.) [S: batch] Good.
When the sounds are blended together to make the word *batch,* the *t* is actually silent. Now let's go through the rest of the words.
The vowels in the words all have short vowel sounds.
You write the letters and read the word.

Go through the words. Call attention to the last four words, which are spelled with just *c-h* at the end, not *t-c-h.*

Do parts 4-6 as described in the instructions on pages 13-14. In part 5, use *which* and *witch* in sentences so that if S. cannot hear the difference, he will know what word to write.

Practice 2-B: Review of Ending Digraphs *-sh* and *-th*

Student's page 5

1

-sh
fish

-th
path

2 What does the word end with?

s sh	t th
1. mis s	1. pat
2. di sh	2. path
3. hu sh	3. bath
4. ga s	4. bat
5. ga sh	5. mat
6. kis s	6. math
7. mas s	7. with
8. ma sh	8. wit

3 Write the letters and say the word.

sh	sh
a sh	di sh
ca sh	wi sh
da sh	hu sh
ga sh	ru sh
ha sh	th
la sh	ba th
ma sh	ma th
ra sh	pa th

4 Read the words.

wish	rash
dish	ash
fish	hash
rush	gash
hush	lash
dash	path
mash	math
cash	bath

5 Write the word you hear.

1. hash	9. wish
2. dish	10. math
3. bath	11. dash
4. gash	12. lash
5. rash	13. fish
6. hush	14. cash
7. mash	15. rush
8. path	16. ash

6 Read the sentences.

Review words: fresh, Smith, burn

1. Fill the dish with nuts.
2. They rush to the bank to cash a check.
3. Fred has a red rash on his hands.
4. Ed takes a bath after his factory work.
5. Can you help Ted with his math?
6. The pups dash up the path.
7. My kids rush into the kitchen, yelling. I tell them to hush.
8. Ted Smith is fixing hash for dinner.
9. I wish we had some fresh fish.
10. The glass cut a gash in her arm.
11. We wish to pay cash for the TV set.
12. Lash the bags to the top of the car.
13. It burned to black ashes.
14. Mash the yams for dinner.
15. Fish is the dish that Mom makes best.

Practice 2-B: Review of Ending Digraphs *-sh* and *-th*

This practice covers two ending digraphs: *sh* and the unvoiced sound of *th.* The only word S. has had that ends with the *voiced* sound of *th* is *with.* S. will not study other such words until later, when he learns long vowel words.

1

T. says: You have seen *s-h* and *t-h* before in words
In this practice, you will review words that have *s-h* and *t-h* at the end.
(Point to *sh.*) What sound does *s-h* make? [S: /sh/] Good.
It makes the same sound at the end of the word as it does at the beginning of a word.
(Point to *fish.*) What is this word? [S: fish] Good.
Can you hear the *s-h* sound /sh/ at the end of *fish?*
Let's review some short vowel words that end with the sound /sh/.

Go directly to part 2. Do the first column, following the procedure in 2-A. Then return to part 1.

T. says: (Point to *th.*) You remember that *t-h* has two sounds, /th/ and /<u>th</u>/.
Most short vowel words that end with *t-h* end with the sound /th/.
Those are the words you will study. Say the sound /th/. [S: /th/]
Good. (Point to *path.*) What is this word? [S: path]
Can you hear the *t-h* sound /th/ at the end of *path*?
Let's go over some short vowel words that end with the sound /th/.
(Go on to the second column of part 2).

Do all the remaining parts of this practice as you have done before.

Practice 3: *bl-*
Student's page 6

1	2 What does the word begin with?		3 Write the letters and say the word.		4 Read the words.	
bl-	b l bl		bl	bl		
lock	1. *bl* ouse	9. *bl* ast	*bl* ack	*bl* uff	bless	blank
block	2. *b* oat	10. *b* ed	*bl* ank	*bl* ush	bled	black
	3. *l* and	11. *bl* oom	*bl* ed		blot	
less	4. *bl* ind	12. *l* ink	*bl* ess		blotch	
bless	5. *bl* eed	13. *b* ond	*bl* ink		block	
	6. *b* ank	14. *l* ame	*bl* ock		blink	
	7. *l* eak	15. *bl* ow	*bl* ot		blush	
	8. *l* ight	16. *b* each	*bl* otch		bluff	

Beginning Blends Practices

The directions and dialog that follow for Practice 3 give you a general pattern to follow for all of the Beginning Blends Practices. You do not have to follow the dialog exactly, but make sure you are very familiar with it and with the suggestions before you begin.

Before starting a practice, read any Note at the top of the practice page. A Note gives additional special directions *for that practice only.*

1

Part 1 introduces each beginning blend. Often S. has not studied words with these blends before.

T. says: This word is *lock.* (Point to first word.) Read *lock.* [S: lock]
Good. (If you know S. has learned these words before, you might ask, "What is this word?" instead of telling him.)
Lock starts with the letter *l,* so the first sound is /l/.
And this word is *block.* (Point to *block.*) Read *block.* [S: block]
The word *block* is just like *lock,* except it has the letter *b* before it. The letter *b* makes the sound /b/, and *l* makes the sound /l/, and when they come together at the beginning, you blend the sounds together to sound like /bl/. Say /bl/. [S: /bl/] Good.

T. says: What is this word? (Point to first word.) [S: lock]
And this word? (Point to second word.) [S: block]
Can you hear the extra /b/ sound in *block*?
Can you hear the *b-l* making the sounds /bl/ at the start of the word?
(Help S. go over these examples again if he has trouble.)
We call the *b-l* together a blend.
You blend the sounds of the letters together to sound like /bl/.
You will see this blend in many words. (Point to the letters of the blend *bl* at the top.)

Repeat the same process with the next words, *less* and *bless.*

For the beginning *s* blends (Practices 7 and 17-22), prolong the *s* sound somewhat as you pronounce the words.

If a practice covers more than one consonant blend, you may want to introduce the first blend and then go directly to part 2, having S. do the auditory discrimination exercise in part 2 for that blend. Then return to part 1 again and introduce the next blend, following with part 2 for that blend. When S. has covered parts 1 and 2 for each blend, go on to part 3. After you have gone over each blend, you might ask S. if he can think of other words that start with that blend.

2

What does the word begin with?

T. says: Now I will read some words. You listen for the beginning sounds.
If the word starts with the sound /b/, write *b* in the blank.
If it starts with the sound /l/, write *l* in the blank.
But if you hear the sound of *b* and *l* blended together, /bl/, write *b-l* in the blank.

Go over the first few words with S. to make sure he knows what to do. Read each word at least twice, clearly and distinctly. You may want to emphasize the beginning sound. It may help S. if he repeats the words after you. S. will have to listen carefully, as many of the words have been chosen because they have minimal pairs; for example, *bleed* is a good word to practice because S. must be able to tell it from *bead* and *lead.*

You should check S.'s work as you go along. S. should do well on this exercise before going on to part 3. If S. seems to have difficulty with this exercise, you should give him more practice with this blend before continuing with the other exercises on this page.

Important: It is assumed that the student has a good knowledge of individual consonant sounds and short vowel sounds. If he does not, he may have difficulty with the remaining parts (3-6) of these practices. You may need to teach or review short vowel sounds for those students needing more practice. *Focus on Phonics 2-A: Short Vowel Sounds* is recommended for this purpose.

3

Write the letters and say the word

In this part, S. will be adding the beginning blend to a word stem made up of a short vowel plus a consonant or consonant digraph. The words are usually grouped together by their short vowel sounds.

T. says: What does *b-l* sound like? (Point to *bl* at top of column.) [S: /bl/]
Good. You can make new words that sound like /bl/ at the beginning.
(Point to *ack.*) *A-c-k* sounds like /ack/. Say /ack/. [S: /ack/]
If I write *b-l* in front of /ack/ (write the letters in), I have the sounds /bl/ and /ack/. Say those sounds as I point to them.
(Point to *bl.*) [S: /bl/] (Point to *ack.*) [S: /ack/] Good.
Can you blend those sounds together into a word?
(Help S. if he has trouble.) [S: black] Good.

Now let's go through the rest of the words.
The vowels in the words all have short vowel sounds.
You write the letters and read the words.

You probably won't have to follow such a detailed procedure with each word. Students who know their sounds and who can blend sounds easily may automatically write down the letters and say the words. Or they may write down the letters and instantly recognize the words without having to blend sounds together. Some students may have great difficulty with this exercise, though. You may need to follow a different procedure in helping them decode the words. For suggestions to help these students, see Appendix A: Helping Students Decode Words with Blends.

The word lists include some common names. S. should be able to identify them immediately by the capital letters. In part 3, only the words that are names have the blends already filled in in S.'s book. Make sure S. does not use capital letters as he writes the beginning blends for the other words. In a few practices, a word is both a name and a common word (example: *Frank, frank*). Words like that are listed both ways in parts 3, 4, and 5.

As S. sounds out the words, you may want to talk about them. You may want to use the words in sentences or phrases that indicate their meanings. If there are several words in a practice whose meaning S. does not know, or if S. has difficulty learning so many words all at once, you may want to circle only the most common words for him to learn. (This is especially true for English as a Second Language students.) If you decide to omit some words in part 3, you should skip over them in parts 4 and 5, too.

There is an excellent reference book you can use to judge word familiarity and the common meanings of words. That book is *The Living Word Vocabulary* by Edgar Dale and Joseph O'Rourke. (It is published by Field Enterprises Educational Corporation, 1976, and distributed by Dome Press, Inc., in Elgin, Illinois.) This national vocabulary inventory gives the precise meanings of words and the grade levels at which they are understood. The words in these practices are limited to those with meanings familiar at sixth grade or before. Only those familiar word meanings are used in the sentences in part 6.

4

Read the words

T. says: Here are the same words that you have been making, in a new order.
Read the words.

As in part 3, the words are grouped together by short vowel sounds, although they are in a new order. If there is more than one blend being studied, the blends are kept separate as they were in part 3.

If S. is learning only part of the word lists, skip over the words he is omitting. Check his reading. Help him if he has any problems (see Appendix A for suggestions). If he has great difficulty with part 4, you should not go on with the practice. Give S. more exposure to those words later, perhaps in a different context.

5 Write the word you hear.

1. blank
2. blot
3. blush
4. block
5. blink
6. blotch
7. bluff
8. bless
9. black
10. bled

6 Read the sentences.

Review word: name

1. Ted fills in the blanks.
2. He says he can win, but he is bluffing.
3. A black family lives in my building.
4. I get red when I blush.
5. Do not blink when I put the drops in.
6. Mom asks God to bless this dinner.
7. Tim's hand got cut. It bled a lot.
8. The gun shot blanks.
9. The black van is blocking our car.
10. Tom blushes when Pam winks at him.
11. Sam blots up the black ink.
12. Write your name in this blank.
13. "God bless you," Dad said to his son.
14. Fred lives two blocks from me.
15. Bob has a red blotch on his neck.
16. My friends are a blessing to me.

5

Write the word you hear

In this part, the words are all mixed, no longer separated by vowel sounds or even by different blends (unless the blends sound exactly alike, as for example, *sc* and *sk*).

T. says: Now I will read each of the words for you. Write the word you hear. (If S. is skipping some words in parts 3 and 4, skip them here too.)

Read the words slowly and distinctly. Repeat them as many times as necessary. S. may want to repeat a word after he hears it. If he misspells part of a word, read the word again, emphasizing the sounds he missed (the beginning, the vowel sound, the ending). For example, if he writes *black* for *block,* you may say, "The vowel sound is different. *Block. Block.*" If S. still has difficulty when you emphasize the sound, you may say, "The vowel sound is /o/. What vowel makes the sound /o/?" Tell S. when the word is a name so he can use a capital letter. Check his capitalization. You may want to help him with his handwriting, too.

You may want to emphasize part 5 for students who are new readers or poor spellers. You can use part 5 as a basic spelling program in which students can learn to spell many words easily. After S. has done a few of the blends practices, you may give him a sheet of paper and ask him to write down words with several blends mixed up together. Then he can review words he has trouble with.

6

Read the sentences

Review Words and New Words that will appear in the sentences are listed at the top. Review Words are mostly from the lessons in *Skill Book 2* or the correlated reader *City Living* of the Laubach Way to Reading series. Students who have gone through *Focus on Phonics 2A: Short Vowel Sounds* will also be familiar with most of these words. If S. has not had a Review Word before, or if he does not recognize it, *tell* him the word.

New Words are usually used at least three times in the sentences.

T. says: Here are some new words you will need in your reading. This word is. . .

Go over the Review Words and the New Words, talking about what they mean and using them in sentences. Point out things to help S. remember the words. Have him write these words. If S. has difficulty remembering or spelling a word, put it on a flashcard for him to review frequently. S. should know these words fairly well before reading the sentences.

It is assumed that S. can read common sight words and short vowel words such as he might encounter in *Skill Books 1* and *2,* the correlated readers, and *Focus on Phonics 2A: Short Vowel Sounds.* In parts 3-5 of the blends practice, S. has had practice reading and writing certain blend words. S. should now be able to read meaningful sentences with the blend words, using the new words, review words, and words he has previously learned.

Several of the blend words have more than one meaning, so the sentences may suggest new meanings of words that you can discuss. You may need to explain some word or sentence meanings to S. if he seems confused. If he is skipping over some of the words in the word lists, you should omit the sentences that have those words until such time as he has learned the words.

In a very few practices, not all the blend words in the word lists are used in the sentences. This is because the words are less common, or because it is too difficult to make sentences with the words available.

Some students may read the sentences with great ease. For others, the sentences will be a challenge. As S. reads the sentences, note the following:

— Does he see the connections between the words he has learned and the sentences he is now reading?

— Does he recognize the most basic sight words easily? Does he need additional practice with some important words?

— Does he know the blend words well? Can he recognize them instantly, or must he sound them out? If he sounds out the words, can he do this well? What methods does he use in decoding words? Does he confuse some words with some other similar words, especially words that differ only in the vowel? What words will he still need practice with? Does he remember words from previous practices?

— What are his skills and strengths in reading?

— Does he understand the way words are used? (Words that have several common meanings may often be used in more than one way. Occasionally, words may be used as different parts of speech, such as *block,* which is used as a noun and as a verb.)

— Does S. comprehend the whole sentence? Does he understand the different types of sentences—statements, commands, exclamations, questions? Does he notice the effect of punctuation? Does he read with expression?

S. may want to go over the sentences several times until he can read them easily. Any student who wants to improve his spelling and handwriting can also *write* the sentences as you dictate them. Because the sentences contain many words from previous practices, S. may first want to review the spellings of the sight words and the blend words he has already had. When he can spell these words easily, he can go on to write the whole sentences. If S. still has trouble with some words when he writes them, you can have him write the words in a list or on cards to review.

If S. writes the sentences, call attention to the use of capital letters for the first word of every sentence and for people's names.

Remember that there is no ideal amount of time recommended for these blends practices. One student may spend several days on one practice, and another may use it as a review and spend ten minutes on it. You must adapt the practices to the needs of your individual students.

Practice 4: *cl-*

Student's page 7

1

cl-

lock
clock

lap
clap

2 What does the word begin with?

c | cl

1. c ot
2. cl oud
3. c amp
4. l uck
5. l ip
6. cl ash
7. cl ay
8. c ause
9. l eave
10. c ub
11. cl ock
12. cl ue
13. l ean
14. l ump
15. cl ove
16. c ap

3 Write the letters and say the word.

cl		cl	
cl	am	cl	ing
cl	ap	cl	ock
cl	ass	cl	ot
cl	ash	cl	ub
cl	ang	cl	uck
cl	ick	cl	utch
cl	iff		
cl	ip		

4 Read the words.

cliff	clap
cling	clang
clip	clam
click	clash
cluck	clot
club	clock
clutch	
class	

5 Write the word you hear.

1. club
2. class
3. cluck
4. clip
5. clot
6. clam
7. cliff
8. clock
9. cling
10. clang
11. clash
12. clap
13. clutch
14. click

6 Read the sentences.

New words: paper, shirt **Review word:** color

1. Pam clips a picture from the paper.
2. Class starts at ten o'clock.
3. They are clapping for the winner.
4. Bob is in the Garden Club.
5. Do not stand on the edge of the cliff.
6. Ed went to the river to dig for clams.
7. That red shirt clashes with this skirt.
8. The clock stopped at six o'clock.
9. Jim writes for his class paper.
10. The lock shut with a click.
11. Put the paper clips in that dish.
12. My wet shirt clings to my back.
13. The clutch on my car does not work.
14. The hens cluck at the chicks.
15. Some birds make nests on cliffs.
16. This color will clash with my shirt.

Practice 5: *fl-*

Student's page 8

1

fl-

lock
flock

lip
flip

2 What does the word begin with?

f l fl

1. f at	9. fl ash
2. fl ake	10. f are
3. l int	11. l oss
4. l ag	12. fl eet
5. fl aw	13. l ick
6. fl ute	14. l ap
7. f ame	15. f og
8. f ight	16. fl ow

3 Write the letters and say the word.

fl	fl
fl ag	fl ing
fl ap	fl ock
fl at	fl op
fl ash	fl uff
fl ed	fl ush
fl esh	fl unk
fl ick	
fl ip	

4 Read the words.

flip	flush
fling	fluff
flick	flop
flat	flock
flash	flesh
flag	fled
flap	
flunk	

5 Write the word you hear.

1. flesh	9. flop
2. flip	10. flag
3. flock	11. flush
4. flat	12. flick
5. flunk	13. fluff
6. fled	14. flap
7. flash	
8. fling	

6 Read the sentences.

Review word: barn

1. The flag is flapping in the wind.
2. What is that flashing in the dark?
3. Tim is flat on his back in bed.
4. Flip a quarter. If it is heads, I win.
5. A flock of birds went by.
6. The farmer fled from the burning barn.
7. Bill is flunking his math class.
8. Put in the letter and lick the flap.
9. It will not flush until I fix it.
10. Jan can do a back flip.
11. Ned flops on his bed.
12. Whip the eggs until they fluff up.
13. Tom is fat. He has a lot of flesh.
14. Jack flicks on the TV.
15. The street is hilly, not flat.
16. Ann flings her ring back at Jim.

Practice 6: *pl-* and *gl-*

Student's page 9

Note: In part 3, the beginning letters are filled in for the student when the word is a name and requires a capital.

1

pl-

lot

plot

gl-

lad

glad

2 What does the word begin with?

p l pl	g l gl
1. pot	1. glaze
2. plump	2. loom
3. pant	3. gum
4. lace	4. glow
5. plead	5. goat
6. plus	6. glove
7. pain	7. land
8. ledge	8. gas

3 Write the letters and say the word.

pl	gl
pl an	gl ad
pl ank	gl ass
pl edge	Gl enn
pl ot	gl um
pl us	
pl uck	
pl ug	
pl um	

4 Read the words.

plot	glum
pledge	glass
plus	glad
plum	Glenn
plug	
pluck	
plan	
plank	

5 Write the word you hear.

1. plug
2. plot
3. plan
4. glass
5. pledge
6. plum
7. Glenn
8. plus
9. glum
10. plank
11. pluck
12. glad

6 Read the sentences. **New word:** plenty

1. Plug in the TV set.
2. I cut my hand on some glass.
3. The men had a plot to rob the bank. We are glad that the plan did not work.
4. Peg looks glum. She misses Glenn.
5. I have plenty of planks to make a shed.
6. Bill looks good with his glasses on.
7. Glenn says the pledge to the flag.
8. Jim plucks a hen for dinner.
9. Ed plans to pledge ten dollars.
10. Kim puts the plug in the sink.
11. The Hills pick plenty of plums.
12. One plus six is seven.
13. Dad is planning his garden. He plans to have corn on this plot.
14. I am glad I have plenty of glasses.

Practice 7: *sl-*

Student's page 10

1

sl-

led
sled

lick
slick

2 What does the word begin with?

s | l | sl

1. sl ope	9. sl ight
2. l ime	10. s ap
3. sl ave	11. l ow
4. s ob	12. s ick
5. l eak	13. sl ing
6. s ang	14. l ump
7. sl ed	15. s ay
8. l ip	16. sl ice

3 Write the letters and say the word.

sl	sl
sl acks	sl im
sl am	sl ip
sl ap	sl ing
sl ash	sl ob
sl ang	sl ot
sl ed	sl ug
sl ick	sl um
sl id	sl ush

4 Read the words.

sled	slum
slot	slush
slob	slug
slam	slip
slash	slid
slap	sling
slang	slick
slacks	slim

5 Write the word you hear.

1. slot	9. slush
2. slick	10. slam
3. slap	11. slid
4. slug	12. slash
5. slim	13. slob
6. sled	14. slip
7. slacks	15. slang
8. sling	16. slum

6 Read the sentences. **New words:** never, down

1. There is slush on the street.
   Do not slip on it.
2. Ann's slacks make her look slim.
3. The shop slashed rugs down to a dollar.
4. My shirt is a mess. I look like a slob.
5. Mom never slaps the children.
6. That sled will never carry four of us.
7. Pam puts on her pink slip.
8. Dr. John put Jim's arm in a sling.
9. If I slim down, my slacks will fit.
10. Put the letters in the slot.
11. Jan never lived in the city slums.
12. Don slammed down the telephone.
13. The children slip on the slick street.
14. My doctor never says slang words.
15. Ben slid down the hill on his sled.

Practice 8: Review of Beginning *l* Blends: *bl-, cl-, fl-, gl-, pl-, sl-*

Student's page 11

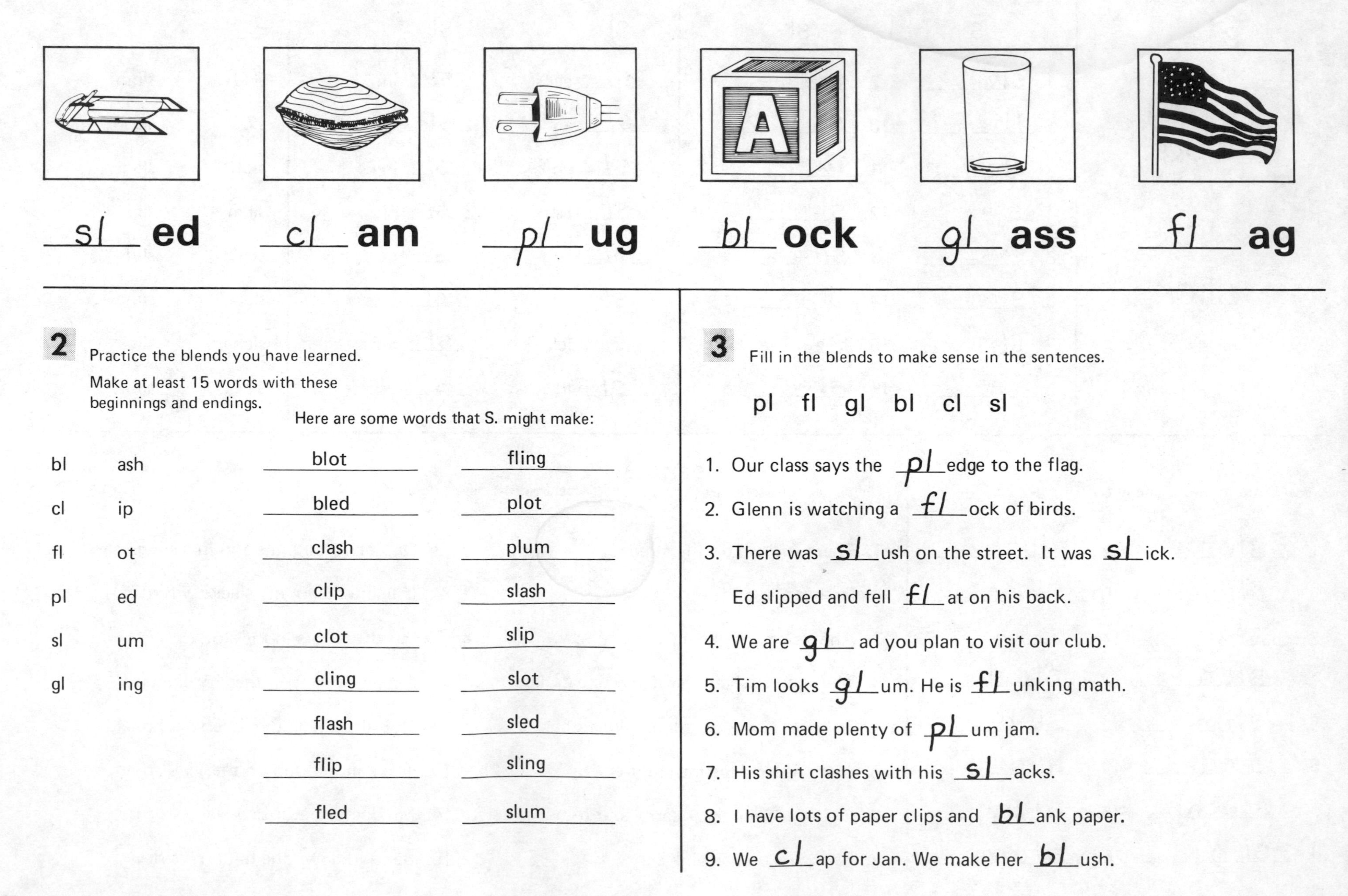

1 Look at the picture and say the word. Then write the letters of the beginning blend you hear.

sl **ed** cl **am** pl **ug** bl **ock** gl **ass** fl **ag**

2 Practice the blends you have learned.
Make at least 15 words with these beginnings and endings.

Here are some words that S. might make:

bl	ash	blot	fling
cl	ip	bled	plot
fl	ot	clash	plum
pl	ed	clip	slash
sl	um	clot	slip
gl	ing	cling	slot
		flash	sled
		flip	sling
		fled	slum

3 Fill in the blends to make sense in the sentences.

pl fl gl bl cl sl

1. Our class says the pl edge to the flag.
2. Glenn is watching a fl ock of birds.
3. There was sl ush on the street. It was sl ick.
   Ed slipped and fell fl at on his back.
4. We are gl ad you plan to visit our club.
5. Tim looks gl um. He is fl unking math.
6. Mom made plenty of pl um jam.
7. His shirt clashes with his sl acks.
8. I have lots of paper clips and bl ank paper.
9. We cl ap for Jan. We make her bl ush.

Review Practices for Beginning Blends

In these practices, S. reviews a number of words he has learned for a particular group of blends. The blends being reviewed are shown at the top of the page. Much of the work involves discriminating between those similar blends.

If S. makes five or more errors on a review, he probably needs more help with those blends. It is important to note the type of error that S. makes. If S. confuses words, are they ones that *look* alike or *sound* alike? Do particular words or blends give him trouble? You may want to test him for vision or hearing problems.

After S. has completed the review practices for particular blends, you can give even more practice reviewing those words by referring immediately to Appendixes B-D. These appendixes give ideas for having S. add endings to blend words he has learned.

1

T. says: What is this? (Point to the picture.) [S: sled] Right.
The beginning blend is missing in the word.
What are the beginning sounds in *sled*? [S: /sl/] Good.
What letters make the blend? [S: *s-l*] Good.
Write those letters in the blank.

Check S.'s work. If S. is not sure, have him pronounce *sled* very slowly, identifying the first sound, /s/, and then the second,-/l/. As you go over each of the words, make sure S. gives the right pronunciation for each word.

2

T. says: Now you will make some blend words.
In this column are the beginning *l* blends that you have studied.
(Point to first column.)
And in this column are endings of words. (Point to second column.)
Put the beginning blends together with the word endings to make real words. The words will be ones you've seen before.
Make as many words as you can. Try to make at least 15 words.
Write the words on the lines below.

Help S. as he makes the words. S. may want to take one beginning blend at a time, matching it with each ending to make possible words.

T. says: Here are some sentences to read. But parts of some of the words are missing. There is a space for each blend that is missing.
You must fill in the right *l* blend to make words that will make sense in the sentence.

S. may immediately recognize the blend necessary to make the word that fits. Or S. may read the sentence, leaving out the word to be filled in, and try to think of the word. If S. cannot guess the word from reading the sentence, he may want to try the *l* blends one by one, to see if they make words and, if so, if the words fit. After S. fills in the correct blend, you may want him to read the sentence again.

Follow this procedure for Practice 16: Review of Beginning *r* Blends and Practice 23: Review of Beginning *s* and *w* Blends.

Practice 9: *br-*

Student's page 12

1

br-

ring
bring

rag
brag

2

What does the word begin with?

b r br

1. b ake	9. r idge
2. br oom	10. b ed
3. r isk	11. br and
4. br ide	12. b oil
5. r oach	13. br ush
6. b an	14. b ag
7. br ain	15. r ace
8. b ook	16. br ave

3

Write the letters and say the word.

br	br
br ag	br ing
Br ad	br ush
br an	
br ass	
br at	
br ick	
br idge	
br im	

4

Read the words.

bran	bridge
brat	brim
brass	
Brad	
brag	
brush	
bring	
brick	

5

Write the word you hear.

1. brush
2. brat
3. brim
4. brass
5. bring
6. Brad
7. brick
8. bran
9. bridge
10. brag

6

Read the sentences.

New words: hair, made

Review words: bread, brother, turn

1. Mom brags, "This is good bread I made."
   She made bread with bran in it.
2. Ben brushes his hair quickly.
3. I cannot carry the bricks up that hill.
4. The bridge is slick when it is wet.
5. Fill my glass to the brim.
6. I brushed the cat's hair from my skirt.
7. Kim brings me some jam for the bread.
8. This dish is made of brass.
9. My little brother is a brat.
10. Brad lives in a big brick building.
11. Bring me a glass of water.
12. The brim of his hat was turned down.
13. "My son is a doctor," he brags.
14. The red truck is on the bridge.
15. Brad has to brush up on his math.

Practice 10: *cr-*

Student's page 13

1

cr-

rib

crib

rack

crack

2 What does the word begin with?

c r cr

1. c ane
2. r ude
3. cr oak
4. c ab
5. r ank
6. cr eam
7. cr ack
8. r ate
9. r ush
10. cr y
11. c ook
12. r aw
13. c ash
14. cr ib
15. cr ust
16. c op

3 Write the letters and say the word.

cr cr

cr ab

cr ack

cr am

cr ash

cr ank

cr ib

cr op

cr ush

cr utch

4 Read the words.

crush

crutch

crash

cram

crab

crank

crack

crop

crib

5 Write the word you hear.

1. crib
2. crank
3. crab
4. crash
5. cram
6. crutch
7. crop
8. crush
9. crack

6 Read the sentences. **New word:** baby

1. The baby is in his crib.
2. Ed got hurt in a car crash.
   A car crushed his leg.
   Ed is on crutches till he gets well.
3. I had to crank up the car to start it.
4. Will you crack the nuts for me?
5. The baby crushed bread in her fingers.
6. Farmers want to have big crops.
7. The brick building fell with a crash.
8. A farmer keeps his corn in a crib.
9. My best pot has a crack in it.
10. When I pack my bags, I cram things in.
    Then my things get crushed.
11. The baby drops the cup and cracks it.
12. We will sell our corn crop.
13. We had crab legs for dinner.

Practice 11: *dr-*

Student's page 14

1

dr-

rip

drip

rug

drug

2

What does the word begin with?

d r dr

1. dr own
2. r ag
3. d ive
4. dr ill
5. r um
6. d ear
7. d unk
8. dr aw
9. r aft
10. d ead
11. dr ain
12. d ip
13. dr eam
14. d ug
15. r ink
16. dr y

3

Write the letters and say the word.

dr	dr
dr ag	dr um
dr ank	dr unk
dr ess	
dr ill	
dr ip	
dr ink	
dr op	
dr ug	

4

Read the words.

dress	drink
drop	drill
drum	
drunk	
drug	
drank	
drag	
drip	

5

Write the word you hear.

1. drug
2. drop
3. drill
4. drink
5. dress
6. drag
7. drunk
8. drip
9. drum
10. drank

6

Read the sentences. **New words:** school, play

1. Drag the boxes out of the shed.
2. He dropped out of school to play drums.
3. Are the men drilling for water?
4. Sam drank so much, he got drunk.
5. Molly's red dress is pretty.
6. Drink plenty of water.
7. That dress is dripping wet.
8. I dropped my fishing rod in the water.
9. She drank every drop of her drink.
10. This school play drags on and on.
11. Water is dripping from the sink.
12. Dr. King locks up the drugs.
13. Don plays the drums after school.
14. She keeps drilling us on our math.
15. We never dress up to go to school.
16. Ed looks drunk, but he is sick.

Practice 12: *fr-* and *pr-*

Student's page 15

1

fr-

rank

frank

pr-

rank

prank

2 What does the word begin with?

f r fr		p r pr	
1.	r ank	1.	p each
2.	fr ee	2.	pr ay
3.	f ill	3.	r obe
4.	f og	4.	pr ide
5.	fr ame	5.	p ick
6.	r isk	6.	r aise
7.	fr ight	7.	p ose
8.	f ail	8.	pr oof

3 Write the letters and say the word.

fr		pr	
fr	ank	pr	ank
Fr	ank	pr	ess
Fr	an	pr	om
Fr	ed	pr	op
fr	et		
fr	esh		
fr	ill		

4 Read the words.

fret	prop
fresh	prom
Fred	press
Fran	prank
Frank	
frank	
frill	

5 Write the word you hear.

1. press
2. frank
3. fret
4. frill
5. prop
6. Fran
7. Fred
8. fresh
9. prank
10. prom
11. Frank

6 Read the sentences.

Review words: friend, pretty, market

1. Press down on it to make it flat.
2. My friends played a prank on me.
3. Fred will get some fresh eggs for us.
4. Let me be frank. This is what I think.
5. The baby frets for her mother.
6. Prop the sick girl up in bed.
7. Frank is pressing his black slacks.
8. Fran's dress for the prom has frills.
9. Max has a fresh fish market.
10. The cops pressed the mob back.
11. Do not fret if you cannot do it.
12. The rack fell down. Prop it back up.
13. The women are good friends.
14. Fran has such pretty dresses!
15. The paper goes to press at six.
16. Get some fresh bread for dinner.

Practice 13: *gr-*

Student's page 16

1

gr-

rip
grip

ram
gram

2 What does the word begin with?

g r gr

1.	gr eed	9.	gr aze
2.	r ace	10.	gr oom
3.	g ain	11.	r im
4.	gr ab	12.	g ate
5.	g as	13.	gr ove
6.	g o	14.	g out
7.	r id	15.	gr ape
8.	r ipe	16.	r ound

3 Write the letters and say the word.

gr	gr
gr ab	gr ub
gr am	gr udge
gr ass	
Gr eg	
gr ill	
gr in	
gr ip	
gr it	

4 Read the words.

grin	grab
grill	gram
grit	
grip	
Greg	
grudge	
grub	
grass	

5 Write the word you hear.

1.	grab	9.	grit
2.	grip	10.	grub
3.	Greg		
4.	grill		
5.	grin		
6.	gram		
7.	grudge		
8.	grass		

6 Read the sentences.

New word: grubby **Review word:** ready

1. Greg grins when he is happy.
2. I grab my bag and run for the bus.
3. Does Frank like grits?
4. Ed is grubby. He fell in the mud.
5. Pat grabs his hand and grips it hard.
6. Fran will cut the grass.
7. Do not carry a grudge.
8. Digging ditches is grubby work.
9. Mom mops up the mud and grit.
10. "Grub is ready! Come and get it!"
11. The baby grins when Dad laughs.
12. Set up the grill on the grass.
    Greg wants to grill the fish.
13. I got grubby working on my car.
14. I want to grab the jug from him.
    But I cannot get a good grip on it.

Practice 14: *tr-*

Student's page 17

1

tr-

rack
track

rip
trip

2 What does the word begin with?

t r tr

1. rack
2. trail
3. trap
4. tuck
5. rust
6. trim
7. rot
8. tip
9. tend
10. trash
11. ripe
12. tree
13. tot
14. ramp
15. tick
16. trace

3 Write the letters and say the word.

tr tr

tr ack
tr ap
tr ash
tr ick
tr im
tr ip
tr ot
tr uck
tr udge
tr unk

4 Read the words.

trot
trunk
truck
trudge
trap
trash
track
trip
trim
trick

5 Write the word you hear.

1. trip
2. truck
3. trash
4. trim
5. trunk
6. trot
7. track
8. trudge
9. trick
10. trap

6 Read the sentences.

1. We want to catch the rats in the trap.
2. Frank runs at the track.
3. Jack plays a trick on Don.
4. Fran will trim Pat's hair.
5. I got a dress for the trip.
   I will pack it in this trunk.
6. Mom put my shirt in the trash.
7. Do not track mud on the rug.
8. The kids trudge up the hill.
   The pup trots after the kids.
9. Trim the fat from the chops.
10. The jack is in the trunk of the car.
11. Do not trip on that trash can.
12. There are car tracks on the grass.
13. She tells her pet to do a trick.
14. That truck is carrying six pigs.

Practice 15: Contrasting *r* and *l*

Student's page 18

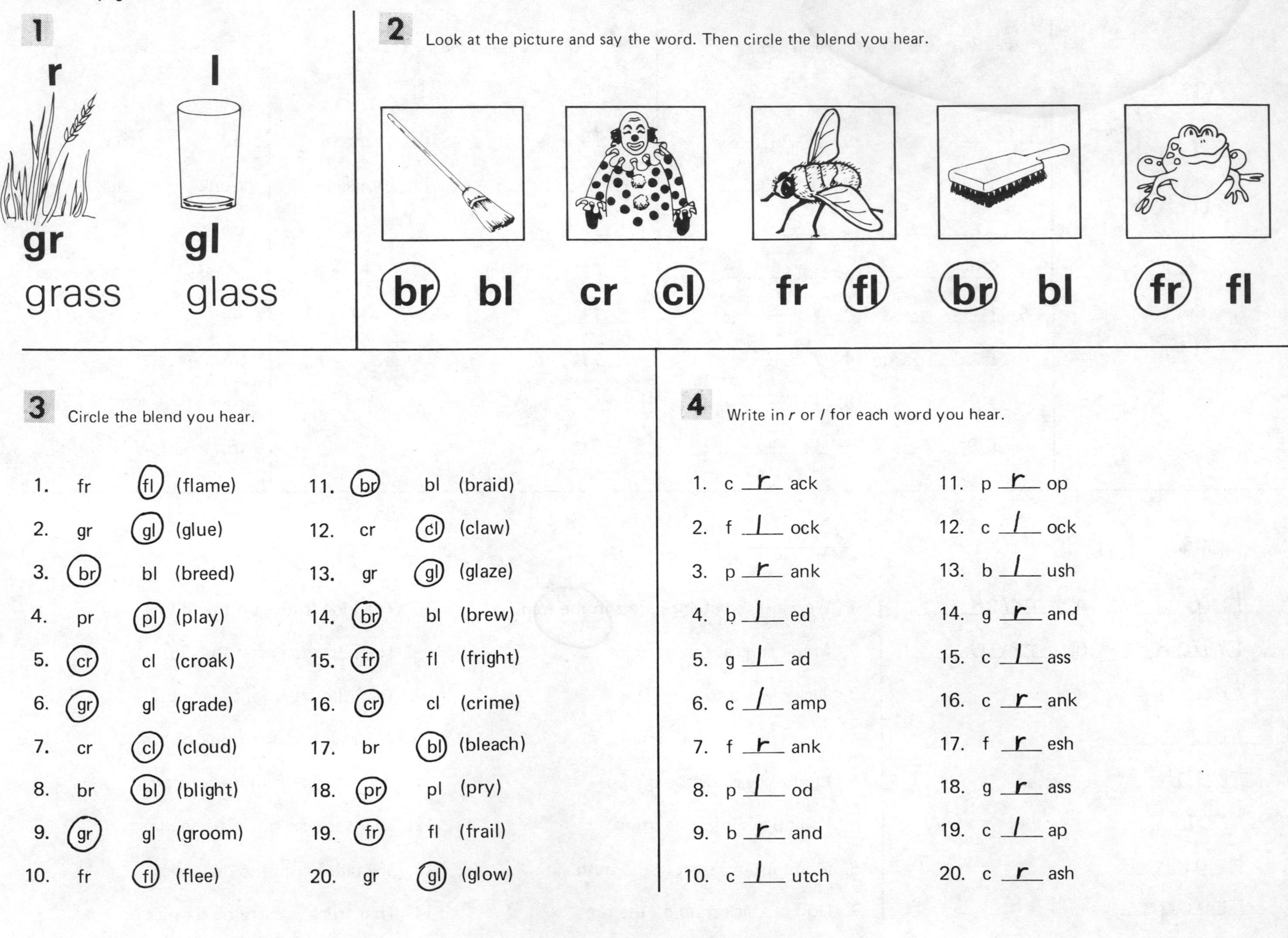

1

r	l
gr	gl
grass	glass

2 Look at the picture and say the word. Then circle the blend you hear.

br bl   cr **cl**   fr **fl**   **br** bl   **fr** fl

3 Circle the blend you hear.

1.	fr **fl**	(flame)		11.	**br** bl	(braid)
2.	gr **gl**	(glue)		12.	cr **cl**	(claw)
3.	**br** bl	(breed)		13.	gr **gl**	(glaze)
4.	pr **pl**	(play)		14.	**br** bl	(brew)
5.	**cr** cl	(croak)		15.	**fr** fl	(fright)
6.	**gr** gl	(grade)		16.	**cr** cl	(crime)
7.	cr **cl**	(cloud)		17.	br **bl**	(bleach)
8.	br **bl**	(blight)		18.	**pr** pl	(pry)
9.	**gr** gl	(groom)		19.	**fr** fl	(frail)
10.	fr **fl**	(flee)		20.	gr **gl**	(glow)

4 Write in *r* or *l* for each word you hear.

1.	c __r__ ack	11.	p __r__ op
2.	f __l__ ock	12.	c __l__ ock
3.	p __r__ ank	13.	b __l__ ush
4.	b __l__ ed	14.	g __r__ and
5.	g __l__ ad	15.	c __l__ ass
6.	c __l__ amp	16.	c __r__ ank
7.	f __r__ ank	17.	f __r__ esh
8.	p __l__ od	18.	g __r__ ass
9.	b __r__ and	19.	c __l__ ap
10.	c __l__ utch	20.	c __r__ ash

Practice 15: Contrasting *r* and *l*

Not all students will need this practice. It is especially designed for students who need more work with the *r* and *l* sounds. People who speak the following languages are most likely to have difficulty with the *r* and *l* sounds: Burmese, Chinese, Dutch, Hawaiian, Japanese, Korean, Micronesian, Samoan, Swahili, Thai, and Vietnamese. (See *Pronunciation Contrasts in English* by Don L. F. Nilsen and Alleen Pace Nilsen; New York: Regents Publishing Company, 1973.) Of course, the difficulty with *r* and *l* is not limited to foreign students.

All of these people may need practice with *r* and *l* at the beginning, middle, and ending of words, but this practice will consider *r* and *l* only in beginning blends. Thus, S. will discriminate between *br-* and *bl-*, *cr-* and *cl-*, *fr-* and *fl-*, *gr-* and *gl-*, *pr-* and *pl-*.

Before starting the practice, you may want to help S. pronounce the *r* and *l* sounds individually. If he is having trouble making the sounds, you might mention that in pronouncing the *l* sound /l/, the tongue tip touches the tooth ridge. In pronouncing the *r* sound /r/, the tongue tip does not touch anything. S. might also want to try pronouncing some of the beginning blends listed in the second paragraph.

T. says: You have studied the beginning *l* blends and the beginning *r* blends. Often people mix up blends when the second letter is *r* or *l*. For example, they confuse *f-r* with *f-l*. This practice will give you more work with those blends that are easy to confuse: *b-r* and *b-l*, *c-r* and *c-l*, *f-r* and *f-l*, *g-r* and *g-l*, and *p-r* and *p-l*.

1

T. says: Here are two words you have seen before.
This word is *grass*. (Point to the word.) Read *grass*. [S: grass]
Grass starts with the *g-r* blend. It sounds like /gr/ at the beginning.
Can you hear the *r* sound /r/ in the blend?
This word is *glass*. (Point to the word.) Read *glass*. [S: glass]
Glass starts with the *g-l* blend. It sounds like /gl/ at the beginning.
Can you hear the *l* sound /l/ in the blend?
Grass. Glass. Can you hear the difference in sound?
Do you see why they are spelled the way they are?
(Go over example again if S. has trouble.)

2

Look at the picture and say the word
Then circle the blend you hear

T. says: Listen for the blend at the beginning of the word.
Then circle the blend that makes the sounds you hear.
(Help S. if he has trouble.) S. may want to repeat the words after you. If so, make sure S. pronounces the words correctly.

3

Circle the blend you hear

T. says: Now I will read some words. You listen again for the blend at the beginning. Circle the blend that makes the sounds you hear.

Go through the first few words with S. to make sure he knows what to do. If S. repeats the words after you, make sure he pronounces them correctly. You may want to correct S.'s mistakes in part 3 before going on to part 4. You can correct mistakes as he makes them, or at the end of this part.

4

Write in *r* or *l* for each word you hear

T. says: This time, I will read some words again, and you will listen for the beginning blend.
The word that I say is written down, except for the second letter.
You fill in that letter—either *r* or *l*—that makes the blend that you hear.

Go through the first few words with S. to make sure he knows what to do. If S. repeats the words after you, make sure he pronounces them correctly. You may want to correct S.'s mistakes as he makes them, or at the end of part 4. If S. misses five or more in either part 3 or part 4, he probably needs additional work with the *r* and *l* sounds in blends.

Practice 16: Review of Beginning *r* Blends: *br-, cr-, dr-, fr-, gr-, pr-, tr-*

Note: For this review, follow procedure on page 21.

Student's page 19

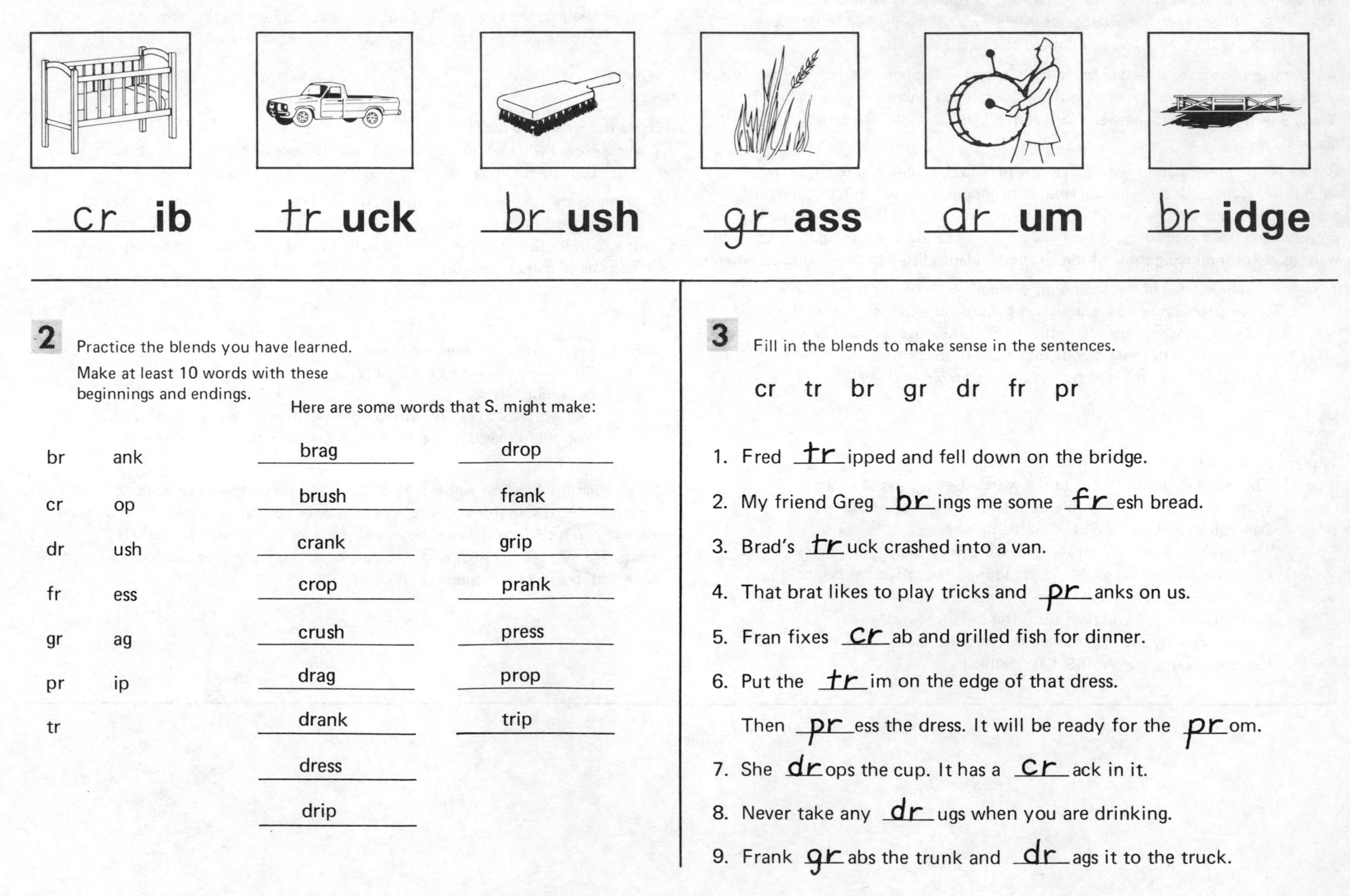

1 Look at the picture and say the word. Then write the letters of the beginning blend you hear.

cr **ib**   tr **uck**   br **ush**   gr **ass**   dr **um**   br **idge**

2 Practice the blends you have learned.
Make at least 10 words with these beginnings and endings.

br	ank
cr	op
dr	ush
fr	ess
gr	ag
pr	ip
tr	

Here are some words that S. might make:

brag	drop
brush	frank
crank	grip
crop	prank
crush	press
drag	prop
drank	trip
dress	
drip	

3 Fill in the blends to make sense in the sentences.

cr tr br gr dr fr pr

1. Fred tr ipped and fell down on the bridge.
2. My friend Greg br ings me some fr esh bread.
3. Brad's tr uck crashed into a van.
4. That brat likes to play tricks and pr anks on us.
5. Fran fixes cr ab and grilled fish for dinner.
6. Put the tr im on the edge of that dress.
   Then pr ess the dress. It will be ready for the pr om.
7. She dr ops the cup. It has a cr ack in it.
8. Never take any dr ugs when you are drinking.
9. Frank gr abs the trunk and dr ags it to the truck.

Practice 17: *st-*

Student's page 20

1

st-

tack
stack

top
stop

2 What does the word begin with?

s t st

1.	st ay	9.	t eam
2.	t ar	10.	st age
3.	s ing	11.	st art
4.	s ag	12.	t ab
5.	st ill	13.	s ale
6.	t ick	14.	st ack
7.	st eep	15.	s eed
8.	s and	16.	s ave

3 Write the letters and say the word.

st	st
st ab	st ill
st ack	st itch
st aff	st ing
St an	st ink
st em	st ock
st ep	st op
st ick	st uck
st iff	st uff

4 Read the words.

stop	stick
stock	stink
staff	stitch
stab	still
Stan	stuff
stack	stuck
sting	step
stiff	stem

5 Write the word you hear.

1.	stuck	9.	step
2.	still	10.	stack
3.	staff	11.	stitch
4.	sting	12.	stuff
5.	stem	13.	Stan
6.	stock	14.	stink
7.	stiff	15.	stop
8.	stab	16.	stick

6 Read the sentences.

Review words: stand, word

1. Ed stops on the steps. He stands still.
2. Our school staff works hard.
3. My finger stings where I cut it.
4. Dad stuffs the hen with bread stuffing.
5. The fudge stuck to the pan.
6. His words were like a stab in the back.
7. I still do not have that hat in stock.
8. The tent is stiff and hard to stitch.
9. Stan keeps the buds fresh.
   He puts the stems in water.
10. Dad stacked the dishes in the sink.
11. Stop playing with that stick.
12. The apples are rotting. They stink!
13. Stan's car was stuck in the ditch.
14. Dr. Bell will stitch up the cut.
15. If your legs get stiff, stand up.

Practice: 18: *sp-*

Student's page 21

1

sp-

pill

spill

pot

spot

2 What does the word begin with?

s p sp

1. spill
2. park
3. send
4. spank
5. soon
6. pin
7. spite
8. say
9. port
10. seed
11. spare
12. pool
13. space
14. spoke
15. soil
16. pot

3 Write the letters and say the word.

sp sp

sp an	sp it
sp at	sp ot
sp ank	sp un
sp eck	
sp ed	
sp ell	
sp ill	
sp in	

4 Read the words.

spot	spit
spell	spill
sped	spin
speck	
spat	
span	
spank	
spun	

5 Write the word you hear.

1. speck
2. spin
3. spat
4. spell
5. spun
6. spot
7. spank
8. spill
9. sped
10. spit
11. span

6 Read the sentences.

1. Can you spell this word?
2. The hot sun makes my head spin.
3. The baby spit up on her dress.
4. Stan spilled his drink on the rug.
   He mopped up the spot with a rag.
5. Jim sped up the street in his car.
6. We made up after our little spat.
7. There are black specks on this paper.
8. Tim spits at his sister.
   Mom will spank him.
9. The baby spun the top.
10. Jack has spots on his glasses.
11. We are having a hot spell.
12. Pam spilled ink on her skirt.
13. What is the span of that bridge?
14. The hot rod spins down the track.

Practice 19: *sn-*

Student's page 22

1

sn-

nag
snag

nip
snip

2

What does the word begin with?

s n sn

1. n ag
2. sn ore
3. s ip
4. n ail
5. sn ack
6. n ear
7. s ub
8. sn eeze
9. s ake
10. n o
11. s ide
12. sn ob
13. s oup
14. sn eak
15. n ap
16. s ort

3

Write the letters and say the word.

sn sn

sn ack
sn ag
sn ap
sn iff
sn ip
sn itch
sn ob
sn uff
sn ug

4

Read the words.

snip
snitch
sniff
snug
snuff
snag
snap
snack
snob

5

Write the word you hear.

1. snip
2. snuff
3. snap
4. snitch
5. snag
6. snob
7. snack
8. snug
9. sniff

6

Read the sentences. **Review word:** snake

1. I snap my fingers and my pup runs up.
2. That snob thinks he is better than we are.
3. I snagged my dress getting in the car.
4. Our children are snug in their beds.
5. A snake is in the tent.
6. That pup is sniffing at our ham.
7. The baby has a snack after his nap.
8. I want some snaps to put on my skirt.
9. Kim snips an ad out of the paper.
10. That shirt is a little snug for me.
11. The man is sniffing. He must be sick.
12. We have apples and nuts for snacks.
13. The snob thinks his car is best.
14. The pup snapped at my friend's leg.
15. Tom snitches his sister's apple.
16. Our plans hit a snag.

1

sm-

mash
smash

mock
smock

2 What does the word begin with?

s m sm

1. sm all
2. s oak
3. m elt
4. sm ack
5. sm ooth
6. s ight
7. m ug
8. sm art
9. s earch
10. m ile
11. sm ear
12. m other
13. s ock
14. s ell
15. sm udge
16. m ash

3 Write the letters and say the word.

sm

sm ack
sm ash
sm ell
sm ock
sm udge

4 Read the words.

smell
smock
smudge
smash
smack

5 Write the word you hear.

1. smash
2. smell
3. smack
4. smudge
5. smock

6 Read the sentences.

New words: smog, smart **Review words:** cover, Smith

1. The car smashed into a bridge.
2. Cars and factories make smog.
3. It is smart to get a good little car.
4. Ed gives Jill a big smack on the lips.
   "You smell good to me," he says.
5. Ron has a smudge on his chin.
6. Jan puts on a smock to cover her dress.
7. The stuff in that trash can smells bad.
8. Smog covers the city.
9. Pat smacked the bug with the paper.
10. Dan Smith thinks he is so smart!
11. There is a smudge on this paper.
12. He smashed the trash down in the can.
13. It is smart to get rid of smog.
14. We can smell the dinner.
    We smack our lips.

Practice 21: *sk-* **and** *sc-*

Student's page 24

Note: Point out that the name *Scott* is spelled with two *t*'s.

1

sk-

kid

skid

sc-

cab

scab

2 What does the word begin with?

s k sk

1. s unk
2. sk y
3. k it
4. sk ill
5. k ey
6. s in
7. sk ate
8. s ip

s c sc

1. sc are
2. s our
3. c orn
4. s ale
5. sc ab
6. s old
7. c uff
8. sc oop

3 Write the letters and say the word.

sk

sk etch
sk id
sk ill
sk im
sk in
sk ip
sk it
sk unk

sc

sc ab
sc an
Sc ott
sc uff

4 Read the words.

skim
skit
skill
skin
skip
skid
skunk
sketch

Scott
scuff
scan
scab

5 Write the word you hear.

1. skit
2. skunk
3. skip
4. sketch
5. skim
6. skid
7. skill
8. skin
9. scuff
10. scan
11. Scott
12. scab

6 Read the sentences.

New word: scatter **Review words:** school, mark

1. That car skids on the wet street.
2. School can help me get job skills.
3. I will sketch a picture of you.
4. The kids scatter when the bell rings.
5. I skip things when I skim a paper.
6. Pam has a new skirt for school.
7. Scott skinned his leg when he fell.
He has a scab where his skin got cut.
8. The wind scatters her sketches.
9. Jack skipped school to go fishing.
10. Frank scans the paper quickly.
11. When skunks get mad, they smell bad.
12. Do not get any scuff marks on it.
13. Mr. Bell is skilled in fixing cars.
14. Our school will put on a funny skit.
15. There is a scatter rug by my bed.

Practice 22: *sw-* and *tw-*

Student's page 25

1

sw-

well

swell

tw-

win

twin

2 What does the word begin with?

s w sw	t w tw
1. w et	1. w ig
2. sw itch	2. t ang
3. s eat	3. tw eed
4. sw ay	4. w ill
5. s ore	5. tw irl
6. w ine	6. tw ice
7. sw eep	7. t in
8. s ift	8. tw inge

3 Write the letters and say the word.

sw	tw
sw am	tw ig
sw ell	tw in
sw im	tw itch
sw itch	
sw ing	
sw ung	

4 Read the words.

swing	twin
switch	twitch
swim	twig
swell	
swung	
swam	

5 Write the words you hear.

1. swell
2. twin
3. swing
4. swam
5. twitch
6. swung
7. twig
8. swim
9. switch

6 Read the sentences.

New word: twenty **Review words:** twelve, watch

1. Ann likes to swim in the river.
2. The twins played on the swings.
3. Jack swung at the bug and hit it.
4. Twelve men and twenty women were there.
5. Twigs and little sticks burn quickly.
6. The twins like to switch jobs.
7. Twenty of my friends will come.
8. A bug bit Ed, and his hand swelled up.
9. There are twelve eggs in that box.
10. A school of fish swam by.
11. Dad swings the baby up in his arms.
12. "Your new dress looks swell," Ed said.
13. Switch on the TV. I want to watch it.
14. Hank swung the bat and got a hit!
15. The pup's leg is twitching.
16. The slacks sell for twenty dollars.

Practice 23: Review of Beginning *s* and *w* Blends: *st-, sp-, sn-, sm-, sk-, sc-, sw-, tw-*

Note: For this review, follow procedure on page 21.

Student's page 26

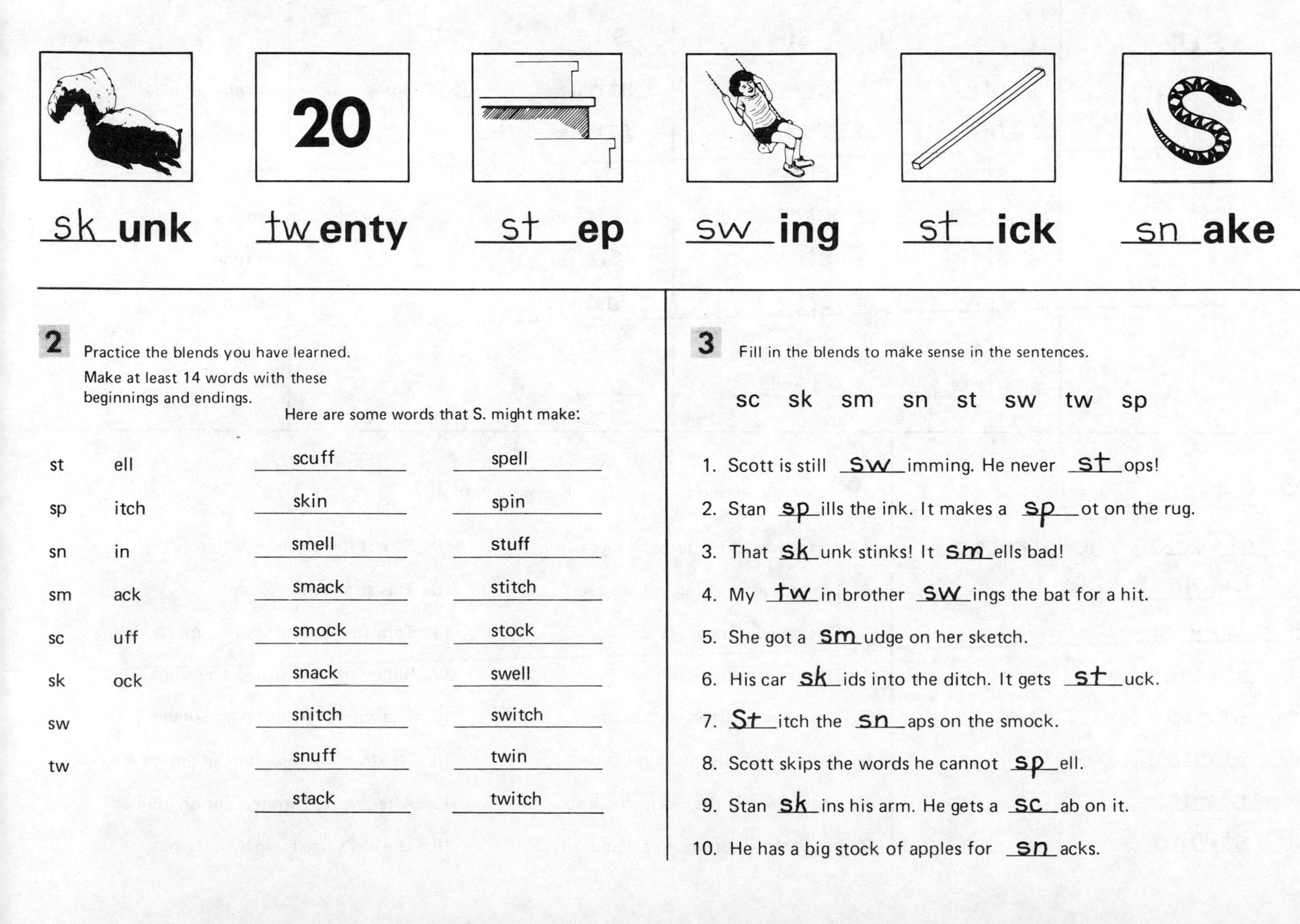

1 Look at the picture and say the word. Then write the letters of the beginning blend you hear.

sk **unk** tw **enty** st **ep** sw **ing** st **ick** sn **ake**

2 Practice the blends you have learned. Make at least 14 words with these beginnings and endings.

st	ell
sp	itch
sn	in
sm	ack
sc	uff
sk	ock
sw	
tw	

Here are some words that S. might make:

scuff	spell
skin	spin
smell	stuff
smack	stitch
smock	stock
snack	swell
snitch	switch
snuff	twin
stack	twitch

3 Fill in the blends to make sense in the sentences.

sc sk sm sn st sw tw sp

1. Scott is still sw imming. He never st ops!
2. Stan sp ills the ink. It makes a sp ot on the rug.
3. That sk unk stinks! It sm ells bad!
4. My tw in brother sw ings the bat for a hit.
5. She got a sm udge on her sketch.
6. His car sk ids into the ditch. It gets st uck.
7. St itch the sn aps on the smock.
8. Scott skips the words he cannot sp ell.
9. Stan sk ins his arm. He gets a sc ab on it.
10. He has a big stock of apples for sn acks.

Practice 24: *str-*

Student's page 27

1

str-

rap

trap

strap

2 What does the word begin with?

st tr str

1. str aw	9. st and
2. tr ain	10. tr ay
3. st ate	11. str ess
4. st eam	12. st ing
5. str ike	13. str ive
6. tr ap	14. str ange
7. st ew	15. tr ip
8. str eet	16. str oll

3 Write the letters and say the word.

str	str
str ap	str ung
str ess	
str etch	
str ing	
str ip	
str uck	
str um	
str ut	

4 Read the words.

strip
stress
string
strut
struck
strung
strum
strap
stretch

5 Write the word you hear.

1. struck
2. strip
3. stress
4. string
5. strap
6. strum
7. strut
8. strung
9. stretch

6 Read the sentences. **Review word:** street

1. Ann stretches her arms and legs.
2. The kids are playing in the street.
3. This string is no good.
4. The red van struck our car.
5. Dan is under stress on his job.
6. Molly straps the pack on her back.
7. I got up when the clock struck six.
8. I have strung up the net. Let us play.
9. Ed cut the paper into thin strips.
10. This strap will stretch.
11. Tom struck a match to burn the twigs.
12. Bill strums the strings and sings.
13. The winner struts up and down.
14. We stress good spelling in our class.
15. After work, I stretch out on my bed.
16. The girl's bag hung by a strap.

Beginning Three-letter Blends

Practices 24, 25, and 26 deal with three-letter blends and digraphs. For these practices, follow the same procedure as for other beginning blends, except for parts 1 and 2, which are slightly different. The instructions below can guide you. Refer to Practice 24, *str.*

1

T. says: You have studied most of the common two-letter blends that are at the beginning of words. In this practice, you will study a three-letter blend, *s-t-r.* In this blend, three sounds are blended together.

(Point to *rap.*) This word is *rap.* Read *rap.* [S: rap]
(Point to *t* in *trap.*) If I add the *t* sound /t/ to *rap,* the *t* sound /t/ and the *r* sound /r/ are blended together to sound like /tr/, and I get the word *trap.* Read *trap.* [S: trap]
Can you hear the difference in *rap* and *trap*?

(Point to *s* in *strap.*) Now if I add the *s* sound /s/ to *trap,* the *s* sound /s/ and the *t* sound /t/ and the *r* sound /r/ are blended together to sound like /str/, and I get the word *strap.* Read *strap.* [S: strap] Can you hear the difference in *rap, trap,* and *strap*?

In Practice 26, the two letters of the digraphs *sh* and *th* make one sound, so you build the *shr-* and *thr-* words in two steps, not three.

2

What does the word begin with?
Part 2 of all three practices is different only in that S. will be listening for two- or three-letter blends, rather than just two-letter blends or single consonants. This will probably be more difficult for him. Make sure S. knows what he is to do.

Practice 25: ***scr-, spr-, spl-,*** **and** ***squ-***

Student's page 28

1

scr-	**spr-**
cram	ring
scram	spring
spl-	**squ-**
platter	quint
splatter	squint

2 What does the word begin with?

scr spl
spr squ

1. scream
2. spread
3. splurge
4. scrape
5. square
6. splice
7. sprout
8. squeal

3 Write the letters and say the word.

scr

scr am
scr ap
scr atch
scr ub

squ

squ int

spr

spr ang
spr ing

spl

spl ash
spl it

4 Read the words.

scrub
scram
scratch
scrap
split
splash
squint
spring
sprang

5 Write the word you hear.

1. scrap
2. split
3. spring
4. squint
5. scratch
6. splash
7. scrub
8. sprang
9. scram

6 Read the sentences.

1. Scrub your hands after you work.
2. I write the number on some scrap paper.
3. Split the apple in two. Give me half.
4. The park is pretty in the spring.
5. I cannot stand cats that scratch me.
   I tell them to scram!
6. The passing car splashed mud on me.
7. This bed has no springs.
8. Mom fed the pup some scraps of ham.
9. The sun makes me squint.
10. We get our water from that spring.
11. Fred scrubs the kitchen with a mop.
12. Ben sprang out of bed at six o'clock.
13. Ted got into the tub with a splash.
14. Sam and Jill will split up.
15. Pam scratched her hand fixing her car.

Practice 26: *shr-* and *thr-*

Student's page 29

1

shr-

rug

shrug

thr-

rush

thrush

2 What does the word begin with?

sh r shr th r thr

	sh r shr		th r thr
1.	shr imp	1.	th ought
2.	sh ed	2.	thr ead
3.	r ank	3.	r ob
4.	shr unk	4.	th umb
5.	sh oe	5.	thr ust
6.	r ug	6.	th aw
7.	shr iek	7.	thr oat
8.	sh ine	8.	r ush

3 Write the letters and say the word.

shr	thr
shr ed	thr ill
shr ill	thr ush
shr ink	
shr ub	
shr ug	

4 Read the words.

shrug	thrush
shrub	thrill
shrink	
shrill	
shred	

5 Write the word you hear.

1. shrill
2. thrush
3. shrink
4. shrub
5. shred
6. thrill
7. shrug

6 Read the sentences.

New word: thread

Review words: three, nurse

1. We have shrubs in our garden.
2. It thrills me when you sing!
3. I want some pink thread.
4. That shrill whistle makes my head hurt.
5. The nurse works till three o'clock.
6. My shirt is ripped to shreds.
7. I ask Kim if this dress will shrink.
   Kim shrugs and says, "What if it does?"
8. We have three children.
9. I snip a bit of thread from my shirt.
10. A thrush is singing in our garden.
11. I get a thrill out of you, baby!
12. Bob cut the paper into shreds.
13. That dress will shrink if it gets wet.
14. Where do you keep your thread?
15. The pup is digging under the shrubs.

Practice 27: Review of Beginning Blends

Note: Three-letter blends are not covered in this review.

Student's page 30

1 Look at the picture and say the word. Then write the letters of the beginning blend you hear.

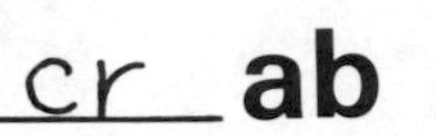

__cr__ **ab**

__st__ **and**

__tw__ **elve**

__pl__ **um**

__br__ **ick**

__sw__ **im**

2 Circle all the words that are the same as the first one.

stiff	fits	sniff	(stiff)	stuff	(stiff)	still	(stiff)
flap	flop	(flap)	flat	flip	(flap)	lap	flip
brag	(brag)	drag	(brag)	garb	bag	grab	bran
spin	spun	(spin)	pins	(spin)	skin	(spin)	snip

3 Draw a line from each blend to an ending to make a word.

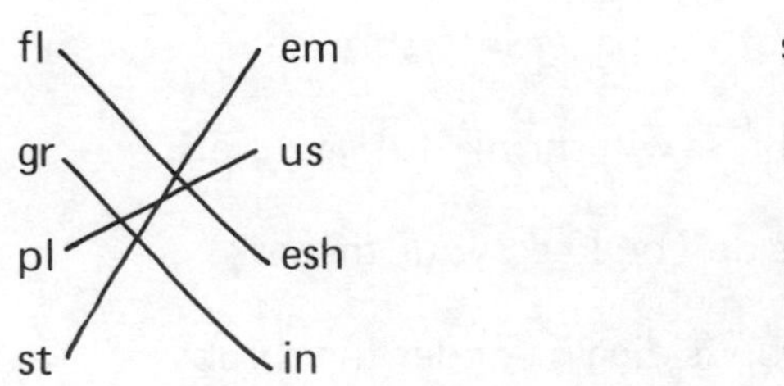

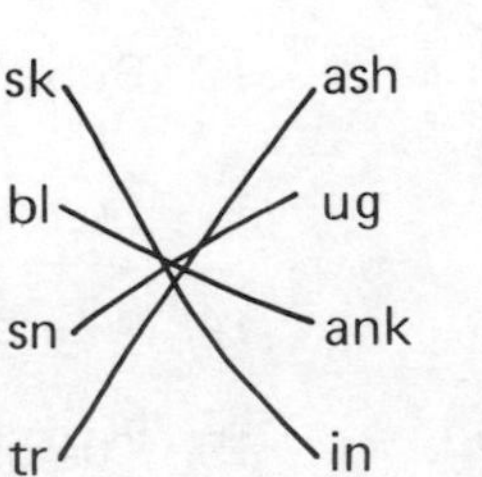

4 Use these words to fill in the blanks:

clutch slim bless brick spit twigs trap swell

1. The school building is made of __brick__.
2. The slacks make you look __slim__ and trim!
3. He __spit__ out the gum and put it in the trash.
4. We want God to __bless__ this dinner.
5. You have to step on the __clutch__ in this car.
6. We plan to catch rats with this __trap__.
7. Pick up the __twigs__ and little sticks.
8. The sting is making my arm __swell__ up.

Practice 27: Review of Beginning Blends

T. says: In this practice, you will review many of the blends you have studied.

1

T. says: Look at the picture and say the word.
Then fill in the letters of the blend you hear.

Be sure S. pronounces each word correctly. S. fills in the missing blend that makes the sounds he hears.

2

T. says: Circle all the words that are the same as the first.
Work from left to right.

This is primarily a *visual* discrimination exercise. It is useful for giving evidence of visual problems like poor vision, directional problems, and reversals of letters and words. It is very important for you to note the kinds of errors S. makes. Some of the incorrect words are new to S., but they *look* like the word to be circled. In a few cases, an incorrect word is the same as the circled word except for the vowel. If S. makes an error by circling these words, he is probably not noticing the vowels in words. If S. makes many mistakes in this visual discrimination exercise (three or more), you should check further for visual problems.

T. says: Now you will match some beginnings and endings of words.
The words have blends that you are reviewing.
There are two groups of words (point to each group).
First do one group of four words, and then the other.
In each group, match the beginnings with the endings to get four real words.
Draw a line from the right beginning to the right ending.
Use each beginning and ending once.
The vowels in the words all have the short sound.
(Help S. blend the sounds together to make words.)

T. says: Here are eight words that you have seen before. (Point to words.)
They have some of the blends that you are reviewing.
Read the words. (Go over the words with S. Make sure S. knows the meanings of the words also.)
Now you will use those eight words in sentences.
Read each sentence and fill in the word that makes sense.
Use each word just once.

Note: These instructions and dialog can be used exactly as is for Practice 43, Review of Other Ending Blends.

Practice 28-A: *-nt*

Note: In part 5, use *sent* and *cent* in sentences so S. will know which word to write.

Student's page 31

1

-nt

ten
tent

plan
plant

2 What does the word end with?

n t nt

1.	de nt	9.	spli t
2.	ra t	10.	te nt
3.	stu n	11.	pai nt
4.	sca n	12.	wi n
5.	cou nt	13.	re nt
6.	rai n	14.	a n
7.	hu nt	15.	fro nt
8.	mi nt	16.	le t

3 Write the letters and say the word.

nt	nt
a nt	le nt
pa nt	re nt
gra nt	se nt
pla nt	te nt
sla nt	ve nt
be nt	we nt
ce nt	spe nt
de nt	

4 Read the words.

lent	rent
vent	tent
bent	pant
sent	slant
dent	grant
went	ant
spent	plant
cent	

5 Write the word you hear.

1.	tent	9.	vent
2.	bent	10.	dent
3.	pant	11.	grant
4.	went	12.	sent
5.	slant	13.	plant
6.	cent	14.	rent
7.	lent	15.	spent
8.	ant		

6 Read the sentences.

New word: aunt **Review word:** twenty

1. Ben sent the rent check to Mrs. Bell.
2. I spent twenty dollars for the pants.
3. Aunt Molly sent me a gift.
4. We have a vent in our kitchen.
5. They are living in a tent by the river.
6. Twenty of us went to work at the plant.
7. I asked Aunt Peg to grant me one wish.
8. Dan was panting as he ran up the steps.
9. Scott lent her twenty cents.
10. My aunt and uncle plant a garden.
11. There are ants and bugs in the tent.
12. That picture is hung on a slant.
13. Ned and Jan are renting a truck.
14. Aunt Pam bent down to look at a plant.
15. Ed got a dent in his car.

    He spent twenty dollars to fix it.

Ending Blends Practices

1

T. says: This word is *ten.* (Point to first word.) Read *ten.* [S: ten] Good.
Ten ends with the letter *n,* so the last sound is /n/.
And this word is *tent.* (Point to *tent.*) Read *tent.* [S: tent]
The word *tent* is just like *ten,* except it has a *t* after it.
The letter *n* makes the sound /n/, and *t* makes the sound /t/, and when they come together at the end, you blend the sounds together to sound like /nt/. Say /nt/. [S: /nt/] Good.

What is this word? (Point to first word.) [S: ten]
And this word? (Point to second word.) [S: tent]
Can you hear the extra /t/ sound in *tent?*
Can you hear the *n-t* making the sounds /nt/ at the end of the word?
(Help S. go over these examples again if he has trouble.)

We call the *n-t* together a blend.
You blend the sounds of the letters together to sound like /nt/.
You will see this blend in many words. (Point to the letters of the blend *nt* at the top.)

Repeat the same process with the next words, *plan* and *plant,* and so on.
In some practices, the contrast is between pairs like *fat* and *fast.* Follow the instructions on page 59 for contrasts like these. In Practice 32: *-ng,* the contrast is between *win* and *wing.* Tell the student that you do not add a /g/ sound to the /n/ sound to say *-ng.* The letters *-ng* together make one sound: /ng/.
In Practice 33: *-nk,* the contrast is between *wing* and *wink.* Tell the student to read the letters *-nk* by saying the sound /ng/ and then adding the sound /k/.

If there is more than one consonant blend covered in the practice, you may want to introduce the first blend and then go directly to part 2 for that blend. Then return to part 1 again and introduce the next blend, following with part 2 for that blend. When S. has covered parts 1 and 2 for each blend, go on to part 3.

When pronouncing words with ending blends, you may want to emphasize both sounds of the blend at the end. For ending *s* blends, you may want to prolong the *s* sound.

2

What sound does the word end with?

T. says: Now I will read some words. You listen for the ending sounds.
If the word ends with the *n* sound /n/, write *n* in the blank.
But if you hear the sound of *n* and *t* blended together, /nt/, write *n-t* in the blank.

Go over the first few words with S. to make sure he knows what to do. Read each word at least twice, clearly and distinctly. You may want to emphasize the ending sounds. It may help S. to repeat the words after you. S. will have to listen carefully, as many of the words have been chosen because they have minimal pairs (example: *pant* is a good word because S. must be able to tell it from *pan* and *pat*).

You may want to check S.'s work at this point. S. should do well on this exercise before going on to part 3. If S. seems to have difficulty with this exercise, you may want to give him more practice with this blend later, before continuing with the other exercises on this page.

Important: It is assumed that the student doing these practices has a good knowledge of individual consonant sounds and short vowel sounds. At this point, he should also be fairly familiar with beginning consonant blends. If he does not know all of these sounds, he may have difficulty with the remaining parts (3-6) of these practices.

3

Write the letters and say the word

In this part, S. will be adding ending blends to single consonants, digraphs, or the consonant blends just covered, plus a vowel (having the short sound). The words are grouped together by their short vowel sounds.

T. says: What does *n-t* sound like? (Point to *nt* at top of column.) [S: /nt/]
Good. You can make new words that sound like /nt/ at the end.
The vowels in the words you will make have the *short* sound.
(Point to *a.*) *A* sounds like /a/. Say /a/. [S: /a/] Good.
If I write *n-t* after /a/ (write the letters in), I have the sounds /a/ and /nt/. Say those sounds as I point to them.
(Point to *a.*) [S: /a/] (Point to *nt.*) [S: /nt/] Good.
Can you blend those sounds together into a word?
(Help S. if he has trouble.) [S: ant] Good.

Now let's go through the rest of the words.
You write the letters and read the word.

You probably won't have to follow such a detailed procedure with each word. Students who know their sounds and who can blend sounds easily may automatically write down the letters and say the words. Or they may write down the letters and instantly recognize the words without having to blend sounds together. Some students may have great difficulty with this exercise, though. You may need to follow a different procedure in helping them decode the words. For suggestions to help these students, see Appendix A: Helping Students Decode Words with Blends.

Refer to the instructions for Beginning Blends, pages 13 and 14, for more detailed directions for parts 3, 4, 5, and 6.

Special Directions for Practices 28-B: *-nt* and 29-B: *-nd*

Both the blends *-nt* and *-nd* have two practices because of the number of words to be used. The second practices should be carried out just like the first except for part 2. In 29-B, part 2 is an auditory discrimination exercise for *-nd* and *-nt*. Here are directions for part 2 of 28-B, *-nt:*

-*nt* words and -*nd* words

T. says: In the last practice, you learned these four words: *bent, lent, sent,* and *spent* (point to the words as you read them).
They are easy to confuse with four other words you will meet in the lesson after this one: *bend, lend, send,* and *spend* (point to the words).
Those two sets of words sound alike, but there are differences.
Listen while I read them in pairs. *Bend, bent. Lend, lent. Send, sent. Spend, spent.* Can you hear that the first word ends with the sounds /nd/, and the second word, which you know, ends with the sounds /nt/? The first word is spelled with *n-d* at the end, and the second word is spelled with *n-t* at the end.

What is the difference in each pair of words, besides ending sounds?
The first word is used to talk about things that happen in the *present,* especially things that happen again and again.
For example: We *send* letters to them. I *spend* a lot of money.
The second word talks about things that are *past*—they have happened, they are finished.
For example: She *lent* me money last week. He *bent* down.
Do you understand the difference? (Answer any questions S. may have.)

That's why it's important to notice whether these words end with *nt* or *nd*. You will see these four *nd* words again in the lesson after this one.

Practice 28-B: *-nt*

Student's page 32

Note: See instructions on page 46 for part 2.

1

-nt

tin

tint

stun

stunt

2 *-nt* and *-nd* words

be**nd**	be**nt**
le**nd**	le**nt**
se**nd**	se**nt**
spe**nd**	spe**nt**

3 Write the letters and say the word.

nt	nt
hi nt	hu nt
li nt	pu nt
mi nt	blu nt
ti nt	gru nt
fli nt	stu nt
pri nt	
spli nt	
squi nt	

4 Read the words.

blunt	flint
hunt	splint
stunt	mint
punt	squint
grunt	hint
tint	
print	
lint	

5 Write the word you hear.

1. print
2. hunt
3. tint
4. flint
5. grunt
6. lint
7. blunt
8. squint
9. stunt
10. mint
11. splint
12. punt
13. hint

6 Read the sentences. **New word:** yard **Review words:** another, want

1. I drop hints for the gift I want.
2. Print your name in this blank.
3. This dress is covered with lint.
4. The stunt man fell and hurt his arm.
   We put a splint on his arm.
5. He can kick a punt very well.
6. Birds hunt for bugs in our yard.
7. That one has a blunt edge.
8. Ann tints her hair red.
9. We will plant mint in our back yard.
10. What do you want? Give me a hint.
11. Do not squint. Put on your glasses.
12. I want some help in our yard.
13. When you shop, get me some flints.
14. The pig grunts as it hunts for nuts.
15. I want another print of this picture.

Practice 29-A: *-nd*

Student's page 33

1

-nd

men
mend

ten
tend

2

What does the word end with?

n d nd

1. wi n
2. be d
3. po nd
4. gra nd
5. fi n
6. ha d
7. sou nd
8. te n
9. mi nd
10. a d
11. Be n
12. hi d
13. blo nd
14. le d
15. sa nd
16. wi nd

3

Write the letters and say the word.

nd	nd
e nd	bo nd
be nd	fo nd
le nd	po nd
me nd	blo nd
se nd	
te nd	
ble nd	
spe nd	

4

Read the words.

pond	bend
bond	spend
blond	tend
fond	blend
mend	
end	
send	
lend	

5

Write the word you hear.

1. tend
2. pond
3. bend
4. end
5. fond
6. lend
7. Spend
8. bond
9. mend
10. blend
11. send
12. blond

6

Read the sentences.

New words: tender, money

Review word: friend

1. Bob lends me money for the trip.
2. Her hands are red and tender.
3. I send letters to friends I am fond of.
4. Mom bends down to pick up her son.
5. Jim tends to spend a lot of money.
   We must put an end to his spending.
6. Pam is mending a rip in the dress.
7. Dad sends Ed to the pond to catch fish.
8. Blend the eggs into the mix.
9. Never send money in a letter.
10. My husband says many tender things.
11. My friend Ben is very fond of blonds.
12. Ned will be happy to tend the kids.
13. They run to the end of the street.
14. Jan spends money on stocks and bonds.
15. Scott gives a tender kiss to Jan.

Practice 29-B: *-nd*

Student's page 34

Note: Part 2 gives special practice discriminating between *nd* and *nt*.

1

-nd

ban
band

win
wind

2

What does the word end with?

nd nt

1.	lend	9.	tent
2.	stunt	10.	wand
3.	blind	11.	kind
4.	and	12.	sent
5.	spent	13.	bond
6.	bent	14.	mount
7.	found	15.	grant
8.	plant	16.	mend

3

Write the letters and say the word.

nd	nd
and	stand
band	strand
hand	wind
land	fund
gland	
brand	
grand	
sand	

4

Read the words.

wind	hand
fund	brand
sand	grand
land	strand
and	
stand	
band	
gland	

5

Write the word you hear.

1.	land	9.	strand
2.	stand	10.	fund
3.	grand	11.	band
4.	and	12.	sand
5.	wind		
6.	brand		
7.	gland		
8.	hand		

6

Read the sentences.

New words: grandmother, Andy

1. Jill has a wedding band on her hand.
2. This land is covered with sand.
3. Wind and water can chap your hands.
4. I can stand up, but I cannot bend down.
5. We had a grand fishing trip with Andy.
6. The school is running out of funds.
7. They cannot land in this bad wind.
8. Grandmother's school is still standing.
9. The kids are playing in the sand.
10. Andy plays drums in the band.
11. Grandmother sends us jams and jellies.
12. My car got stuck, and I was stranded.
13. I cannot stand this wind!
14. Grandmother is mending Andy's shirt.
15. Hand me that can of corn.
I like that brand.

Practice 30: *-nch*

Student's page 35

1

-nch

pin
pinch

bran
branch

2 What does the word end with?

n ch nch

1. bru nch
2. mu ch
3. tre nch
4. it ch
5. bra n
6. be nch
7. crut ch
8. pu n
9. cle nch
10. pit ch
11. lu nch
12. ra n
13. que nch
14. hut ch
15. bu n
16. wret ch

3 Write the letters and say the word.

nch	nch
ra nch	bu nch
bra nch	hu nch
be nch	lu nch
que nch	mu nch
dre nch	pu nch
tre nch	cru nch
i nch	
pi nch	

4 Read the words.

drench	bunch
trench	munch
quench	pinch
bench	inch
hunch	ranch
punch	branch
lunch	
crunch	

5 Write the word you hear.

1. lunch
2. drench
3. ranch
4. punch
5. quench
6. inch
7. bench
8. trench
9. branch
10. munch
11. pinch
12. crunch
13. bunch
14. hunch

6 Read the sentences.

Review word: valley

1. We have a big ranch in the valley.
2. I have a hunch that Jack wants to go.
3. I fell in the water and got drenched.
4. When I pinched her arm, she yelled.
5. A bunch of us work at a branch office.
6. Take up the pants an inch and a half.
7. Andy made some punch for our lunch.
8. The apple crunched when he bit into it.
9. The batter went back to the bench.
10. A bunch of branches fell in our yard.
11. That car missed me by inches.
12. I have a hunch I am going to win.
13. The ranch hands stop work for lunch.
14. I picked up an apple to munch on.
15. Stan punched in at seven o'clock.
16. She digs a trench in her yard.

Practice 31: *-nce, -nse,* **and** *-nge*

Student's page 36

Note: Tell S. that *-nce* and *-nse* make the same sound. Note that in part 2, S. works only with *-nce*, not *-nse*. In part 5, tell S. where *-nce* words stop and *-nse* words begin.

1

-nce
sin
since

-nse
ten
tense

-nge
twin
twinge

2 What does the word end with?

n nce	n nge
1. da nce	1. bi n
2. fe nce	2. stra nge
3. he n	3. lou nge
4. si nce	4. spu n
5. wi n	5. cri nge
6. cha nce	6. ra nge
7. pri nce	7. twi n
8. te n	8. plu nge

3 Write the letters and say the word.

nce	nse
da nce	se nse
cha nce	te nse
gla nce	ri nse
tra nce	**nge**
fe nce	hi nge
si nce	fri nge
pri nce	plu nge

4 Read the words.

fence	rinse
prince	sense
since	tense
chance	
trance	plunge
dance	fringe
glance	hinge

5 Write the word you hear.

1. since
2. glance
3. dance
4. fence
5. prince
6. chance
7. trance
8. rinse
9. tense
10. sense
11. fringe
12. plunge
13. hinge

6 Read the sentences. **New word:** once

1. Jan puts up a fence to keep her pup in.
2. He wants a chance to dance with her.
3. I glance at the clock and rush to work.
4. Will you fix the hinge on my trunk?
5. I went to a dance there once.
6. It is good sense not to take chances.
7. I rinse my hair with hot water.
8. Jill has danced since she was six.
9. They plunge into the river to swim.
10. That does not make sense to me.
11. I danced with a prince once.
12. She looks like she is in a trance.
13. A red fence hid the trash cans.
14. I get tense when the kids yell.
15. Once I had a chance to marry Pat.
16. Ann put a fringe on her skirt.

Practice 32: *-ng*
Student's page 37

Note: To read the letters *-ng,* you do not say /n/ and then add /g/. The letters *-ng* together make one sound: /ng/.

1

-ng

win
wing

ban
bang

2 What does the word end with?

n g ng

1.	ra g	9.	bri ng
2.	spri ng	10.	sa g
3.	ba ng	11.	lu ng
4.	wi g	12.	pa n
5.	ru n	13.	ta g
6.	ga ng	14.	su n
7.	si ng	15.	thi n
8.	fa n	16.	hu g

3 Write the letters and say the word.

ng	ng
ba ng	bri ng
ga ng	sli ng
ha ng	sti ng
ki ng	swi ng
ri ng	spri ng
si ng	stri ng
wi ng	hu ng
thi ng	lu ng

4 Read the words.

ring	sing
thing	swing
sting	spring
king	lung
sling	hung
bring	gang
wing	bang
string	hang

5 Write the word you hear.

1.	wing	9.	sing
2.	sting	10.	king
3.	hang	11.	thing
4.	sling	12.	spring
5.	lung	13.	bang
6.	bring	14.	hung
7.	string	15.	swing
8.	gang	16.	ring

6 Read the sentences.

New word: something **Review word:** finger

1. The ring does not fit my finger.
2. Bob hangs out with a street gang.
3. I think something is stinging me!
4. Andy hung up the telephone.
5. The doctor put Ed's arm in a sling.
6. Bring me something to put on.
7. He has a big string of fish.
8. Jack will sing at the spring dance.
9. The king asks for something to drink.
10. Scott bangs on his drums.
11. They fix the wing of the jet.
12. We stop work when the bell rings.
13. A gang of kids plays on the swings.
14. Smog hurts your lungs.
15. The picture is hanging by a string.
16. The King Family sings on TV.

Practice 33: *-nk*

Student's page 38

Note: To read the letters *-nk*, say the sound /ng/ and then add the sound /k/.

1

-nk

wing
wink

bang
bank

2 What does the word end with?

n k nk

1.	ba nk	9.	pi nk
2.	ra n	10.	slic k
3.	duc k	11.	wi n
4.	li nk	12.	stu n
5.	stic k	13.	cra nk
6.	si n	14.	tru nk
7.	tac k	15.	bri nk
8.	bu n	16.	thic k

3 Write the letters and say the word.

nk	nk
ba nk	wi nk
ra nk	thi nk
ta nk	dri nk
ya nk	sti nk
li nk	shri nk
pi nk	bu nk
ri nk	du nk
si nk	ju nk

4 Read the words.

wink	drink
pink	dunk
stink	junk
think	bunk
link	yank
sink	rank
rink	bank
shrink	tank

5 Write the word you hear.

1.	yank	9.	wink
2.	sink	10.	junk
3.	dunk	11.	tank
4.	link	12.	drink
5.	stink	13.	bunk
6.	pink	14.	shrink
7.	bank	15.	rank
8.	rink	16.	think

6 Read the sentences.

Review words: past, thank, Frank, Hank

1. I think we have money in the bank.
2. Frank winks at Peg.
3. Do not dunk that pot in water.
4. He ranks number one in my class.
5. Thanks for giving us the bunk beds.
6. I think that is funny!
7. Put this junk in the trash can.
8. Hank drinks a glass of water.
9. The fish sinks in the tank.
10. She fell down at the rink.
11. Fill out this pink slip.
12. My pants will shrink if they get wet.
13. This trash stinks!
14. He yanks the paper out of my hands.
15. Grandmother is my link with the past.
16. Thanks for filling up the gas tank.

Practice 34: More Practice with *-ng* and *-nk*

Student's page 39

1

-ng	-nk
wing	wink
bang	bank
sung	sunk

What does the word end with?

-ng -nk

1. cli ng
2. ta ng
3. ho nk
4. ra nk
5. su ng
6. ki ng
7. bla nk
8. ha ng
9. bri nk
10. stro ng
11. stu nk
12. you ng
13. sa nk
14. sli ng
15. wi nk
16. ga ng
17. lu ng
18. thi nk
19. chu nk
20. spri ng
21. wro ng
22. sti nk
23. cla ng
24. tru nk
25. fla nk
26. si ng
27. flu ng
28. ya nk
29. ri nk
30. hu nk
31. ba ng
32. pi nk

2

The **present** is used for things that happen again and again.

I **sing** every day.

The **past** is used for things that happened and are finished.

I **sang** yesterday.

And some forms of these words are used with **has** or **have.**

I **have sung** since I was ten.

Every day	Yesterday	has/have +
ring	rang	rung
sing	sang	sung
spring	sprang	sprung
drink	drank	drunk
sink	sank	sunk
stink	stank	stunk
shrink	shrank	shrunk
cling	clung	clung
fling	flung	flung
sting	stung	stung
string	strung	strung
swing	swung	swung
hang	hung	hung

3

Use the **past** of the word.

sink 1. The ship sank yesterday.

hang 2. We hung up the picture.

fling 3. She flung her bag down.

ring 4. My telephone rang.

string 5. They strung up the net.

cling 6. Jimmy clung to my hand.

drink 7. The baby drank from a cup.

spring 8. Dad sprang out of bed.

Use the word that goes with **has** or **have.**

ring 1. The bell for class has rung.

hang 2. He has hung up his shirt.

sing 3. We have sung at dances.

shrink 4. The dresses have shrunk.

drink 5. Jim has drunk some water.

stink 6. The trash has stunk for days.

swing 7. Bob has swung the bat.

sting 8. No bugs have stung us.

Practice 34: More Practice with *-ng* and *-nk*

T. says: Now you have studied many words that end with *n-g* and *n-k.* This practice will give you help in telling the sounds apart. It will also introduce you to many *n-g* and *n-k* words you haven't had before.

1

T. says: Let's practice the sounds first. (Point to *-ng.)* Remember that *n-g* makes the sound /ng/. Say the sound /ng/. [S: /ng/] Good. (Point to *nk.*) And *n-k* is made up of the sound /ng/, plus the sound /k/. So *n-k* sounds like /nk/. Say /nk/. [S: /nk/] Good.

These pairs of words will help you tell the sounds apart. (Point to *wing.*) What is this word? [S: wing] Good. (Point to *wink.*) And this one? [S: wink] Yes. Can you hear the difference in the ending sounds?

Help S. if he has trouble. Repeat this process for *bang* and *bank* and *sung* and *sunk.*

What does the word end with?

T. says: Now I will read some words. You listen for the ending sounds. If the word ends with the *n-g* sound /ng/, write *n-g* in the blank. If it ends with the *n-k* sounds /nk/, write *n-k* in the blank.

Go through the first few words with S. to make sure he knows what to do. If S. repeats the words after you, make sure he pronounces them correctly. You may want to correct S.'s mistakes in this part before going on to part 2. You can correct them as he makes them, or at the end of the part.

2

T. says: Now you will learn many *n-g* words and *n-k* words that are similar to the ones you already know. Only the vowels are different. Look at the chart of words below. (Point to chart.) These words describe *actions*—they tell about things that are *happening.* This first column of words (point to first column) tells about things that are happening in the *present* time (point to explanation at top of part 2). These words are used to tell about things that happen every day. For example: "I *sing* every day." The second column (point to second column) tells about things that have happened, that are finished, or *past* (point to the explanation). For example: "I *sang* yesterday."

T. says: Sometimes you need a third word if you are using *has* or *have* (point to third column). For example: "I have *sung* since I was ten." (Point to the explanation.) You are using the word *have,* so you must use *sung* after it. All of those words—*sing, sang,* and *sung*—tell about the same kind of action. But *sing* is used for the present time, *sang* is used for the past time, and *sung* is used after *has* and *have.* Let's look at other words that go together like *sing, sang,* and *sung.* Only the vowels are different in the words.

Go through the list of words, encouraging S. to sound out the words himself. Talk about what the words mean, and use them in sentences with the words *every day, yesterday,* and *has* and *have.* Point out that for the last six words on the list, the past form is the same as the word to be used after *has* and *have.* Encourage S. to make up his own sentences with the words.

3

Use the *past* of the word

T. says: Now you have learned the *past* of some common words. Look at each word that comes before the sentences. Write the past form of that word in the blank. Then read the sentence.

Help S. if he needs it, letting him refer to the chart in part 2 if he forgets the words. Check S.'s work.

Use the word that goes with *has* or *have*

T. says: Now look at the word that comes before the sentences. In the blank, write the form of that word that goes with *have* or *has.* Then read the sentence.

Help S. if he needs it. Check his work.

Practice 35: Review of Ending *n* Blends: *-nt, -nd, -nch, -nge, -nce, -nse, -ng, -nk*

Student's page 40

1 Look at the picture and say the word. Then write the letters of the ending blend you hear.

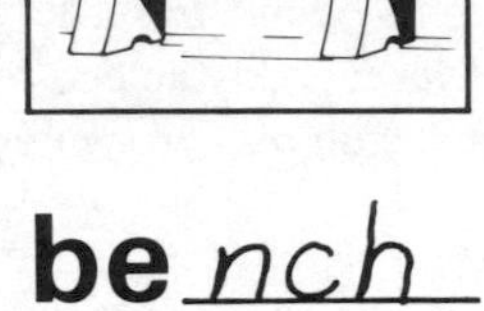

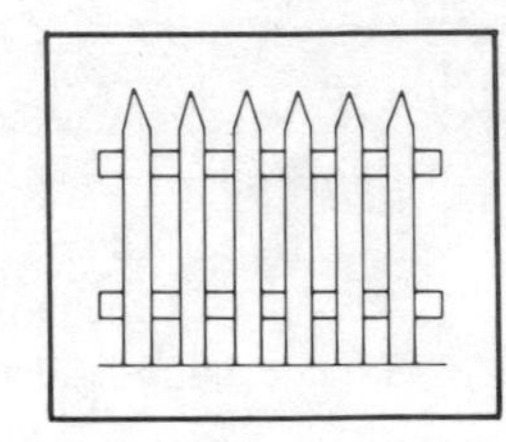

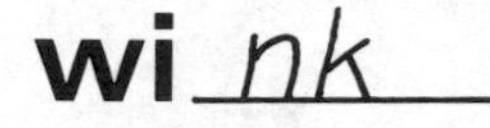

wi nk **a** nt **be** nch **ki** ng **ba** nd **fe** nce

---

2 Practice the blends you have learned.
Make at least 12 words with these beginnings and endings.

pu	nd
wi	nt
ra	nch
be	ng
hu	nk

Here are some words that S. might make:

bench	punk
bend	punt
bent	ranch
hunch	rang
hung	rank
hunk	wind
hunt	wing
punch	wink

3 Fill in the blends to make sense in the sentences.

nk nt nch nce nse nd nge ng

1. Andy's aunt went out to lu nch and spent twenty dollars.
2. This bunch of numbers makes no se nse to me.
3. She has tended the pla nt s since spring.
4. The ga ng hangs out at the ranch every cha nce they get.
5. Tha nk you for bringing me some punch to dri nk.
6. The blo nd girl can sing and da nce.
7. I think I will take a plu nge in the river.
8. Give me a ha nd. I will pitch this tent on the sa nd.
9. The pi nk pants are covered with li nt.
10. I spe nt the funds. But the bank can le nd me money.

Practice 35: Review of Ending *n* Blends

1

Look at the picture and say the word
Then write the letters of the ending blend you hear

T. says: What is this? (Point to picture.) [S: wink]
The ending blend is missing in the word.
What sounds does *wink* end with? [S: /nk/] Good.
What letters make the sounds /nk/? Write the letters in the blank.

For the word *king,* ask about the *sound* it ends with rather than the *sounds,* since the letters *-ng* together make one sound, /ng/.

For the word *fence,* ask "What letters make the sounds /ns/ in *fence*?"

Check S.'s work. As you go over each of the words, make sure S. gives the correct pronunciation.

Practice the blends

T. says: Now you will make some blend words.
In this column are some ending *n* blends that you have studied.
(Point to second column.)
And in this column are beginnings of words. (Point to first column.)
Put the word beginnings together with the ending blends to make real words. The words will be ones you've seen before.
Make as many words as you can. Try to make at least 12 words.
Write the words on the lines below.

Help S. as he makes the words. S. may want to take one ending blend at a time, matching it with each beginning to make possible words.

Fill in the blends to make sense in the sentence

T. says: Here are some sentences to read. But parts of some of the words are missing. There is a space for each blend that is missing.
You must fill in the right *n* blend to make words that will make sense in the sentence.

S. may immediately recognize the blend necessary to make the word that fits. Or S. may read the sentence, leaving out the word to be filled in, and try to think of the word. If S. cannot guess the word from reading the sentence, he may want to try the *n* blends one by one, to see if they make words and, if so, if the words fit. After S. fills in the correct blend, you may want him to read the sentence again.

You may want to refer to Appendixes B-D for ideas for endings practices.

Practice 36: ***-mp***

Student's page 41

1

-mp

dam
damp

bum
bump

2 What does the word end with?

m p mp

1. da mp	9. stu mp
2. swa p	10. hu m
3. shri mp	11. la p
4. cla m	12. thu mp
5. lu mp	13. ski mp
6. cha p	14. slu m
7. plu m	15. tra p
8. pu p	16. ra m

3 Write the letters and say the word.

mp	mp
ca mp	li mp
da mp	shri mp
la mp	bu mp
ra mp	du mp
cha mp	lu mp
cra mp	plu mp
tra mp	stu mp
sta mp	pu mp

4 Read the words.

lump	ramp
stump	camp
pump	stamp
dump	lamp
bump	tramp
plump	damp
shrimp	champ
limp	cramp

5 Write the word you hear.

1. dump	9. champ
2. lamp	10. tramp
3. stamp	11. lump
4. pump	12. damp
5. camp	13. cramp
6. ramp	14. shrimp
7. limp	15. plump
8. stump	16. bump

6 Read the sentences.

Review word: jump

1. At camp, we get water from a pump.
2. Take that lamp to the dump.
3. Don has a cramp in his leg.
   It makes him limp.
4. This letter has no stamp on it.
5. Tom bumped his head and got a big lump.
6. Ned dumps the shrimp in a pan.
7. I jump in my car and head for our camp.
8. I will dig up the stump in my yard.
9. We hung up the damp shirts.
10. There are bumps in our street.
11. Jim is plump. He wants to be thin.
12. Rub the lamp with a damp rag.
13. We look like tramps.
14. He is the winner and still champ!
15. The car got on the ramp.

Other Ending Blends

For the remaining blends practices, follow the same procedures as for the previous ending blends, except for parts 1 and 2 in these exercises: 37-A, 37-B, 41, and 42.

Follow this procedure for part 1 of these exercises. (This one is for Practice 37-A.)

1

T. says: This word is *fat.* (Point to first word.) Read *fat.* [S: fat] Good.
Fat ends with the letter *t,* so the last sound is /t/.
And this word is *fast.* (Point to *fast.*) Read *fast.* [S: fast]
The word *fast* is just like *fat,* except it has an *s* before the *t.*
The letter *s* makes the sound /s/, and *t* makes the sound /t/, and when they come together at the end, you blend the sounds together to sound like /st/.

Say the blend /st/. [S: /st/] Good.
What is this word? (Point to first word.) [S: fat]
And this word? (Point to second word.) [S: fast]
Can you hear the extra *s* sound in *fast*?
Can you hear the *s-t* making the blend /st/ at the end of the word?
(Help S. with the words again if he has trouble. Go over the other examples.)

2

Circle the word you hear

Part 2 of these practices is designed to help S. discriminate between frequently confused ending sounds.

Follow this procedure. (This one is for Practice 37-B.)

T. says: You have been studying the ending blend *s-t.*
The *s-t* blend is often confused with *t-s* at the end of words.
This exercise will help you tell the difference.
I will read some words. Listen for the sounds at the end of each word.
If it sounds like the word has the *s-t* blend /st/ at the end, circle the word on the right.
If it sounds like the word ends with *t-s,* /ts/, circle the word on the left.
Ready? *Nets. Nets.*

Read each word slowly at least twice. It may help S. to repeat the words after you. If he does, make sure he pronounces each one correctly. If S. has trouble with the first word, contrast *nets* with *nest,* explaining the difference.

If S. has much difficulty with this part, he may need more exercises like this one to practice. As there is a very limited number of actual words that can be contrasted in this way, you may have to use nonsense words. This confusion of the *s* sounds at the end is common with the ending blends *-st, -sk,* and *-sp.* If you would like to give S. practice with *-sk* and *-sp,* give him this exercise:

Circle the word you hear.

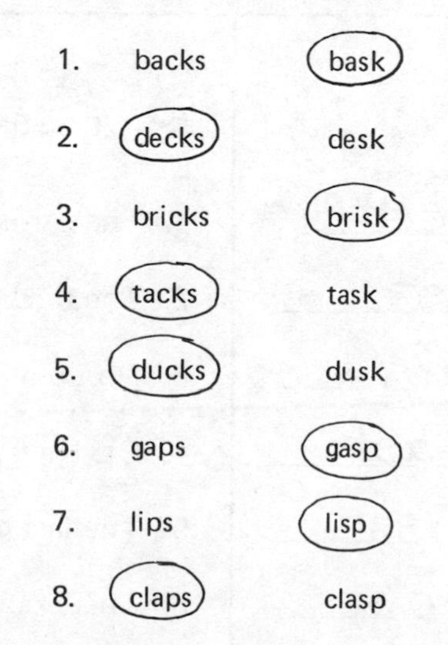

Practice 37-A: *-st*

Student's page 42

Note: Point out that *guest* is spelled with a *u*.

1

-st

fat
fast

pet
pest

2 What does the word end with?

s t st

1.	ju st	9.	mis s
2.	pas s	10.	ve t
3.	li t	11.	la st
4.	mi st	12.	gues s
5.	we t	13.	cru st
6.	les s	14.	pe st
7.	ca st	15.	los s
8.	ru t	16.	pa t

3 Write the letters and say the word.

st	st
ca st	gue st
fa st	ne st
la st	pe st
ma st	re st
pa st	te st
va st	ve st
bla st	we st
be st	che st

4 Read the words.

test	pest
nest	last
chest	cast
guest	mast
vest	blast
best	fast
west	vast
rest	past

5 Write the word you hear.

1.	west	9.	guest
2.	last	10.	fast
3.	rest	11.	test
4.	cast	12.	blast
5.	chest	13.	vest
6.	vast	14.	mast
7.	best	15.	pest
8.	past	16.	nest

6 Read the sentences.

New word: day **Review word:** left

1. The car is headed west, going fast.
2. The bird builds a nest out of twigs.
3. Do your best on the rest of the test.
4. Dr. King put my leg in a cast.
5. The last guest left at half past ten.
6. This brand of pest killer is the best.
7. Ted ran fast. He ran past the shop.
8. Dan's ranch out west is vast.
9. He will test that car last.
10. Put this red vest in the chest.
11. The ship has a big mast.
12. No one was hurt in the blast.
13. I will fast for the rest of the day.
14. Our guest wants to rest.
15. Ed's chest hurts.
 Dr. Bell tells him to rest.

Practice 37-B: *-st*

Student's page 43

Note: Instructions for part 2 are on page 59.

1

-st

lit
list

rut
rust

2

Circle the word you hear.

1. (nets) nest
2. fits (fist)
3. vets (vest)
4. ruts (rust)
5. (bets) best
6. (pats) past
7. (cats) cast
8. wets (west)

3

Write the letters and say the word.

st st

fi	st	mu	st
li	st	ru	st
mi	st	cru	st
twi	st	tru	st
bu	st		
du	st		
gu	st		
ju	st		

4

Read the words.

just	mist
rust	fist
bust	twist
must	list
trust	
gust	
crust	
dust	

5

Write the word you hear.

1. must
2. gust
3. rust
4. list
5. just
6. trust
7. fist
8. dust
9. twist
10. crust
11. mist
12. bust

6

Read the sentences. **New word:** off **Review word:** sister

1. Cut the crusts off the bread.
2. Dusting is the last job on my list.
3. My car has just started to rust.
4. This thread is twisted.
5. You must have trust in your friends.
6. He punched the bag with his fists.
7. A gust of wind carried off my hat.
8. There is just one test I must take.
9. A thick mist covered the pond.
10. Mr. Hill set up a trust fund.
11. I must make out a shopping list.
12. Put the apple filling into the crust.
13. My sister just dusted off the chest.
14. The pot was covered with rust.
15. You can trust that judge to be just.
16. Dan twisted the lid off the jar.

Practice 38: *-sk* and *-sp*

Student's page 44

1

-sk

mass
mask

-sp

gas
gasp

2 What does the word end with?

s k sk s p sp

1.	tuc k	1.	clas s
2.	du sk	2.	whi p
3.	mas s	3.	cri sp
4.	bric k	4.	li p
5.	fla sk	5.	ga s
6.	dec k	6.	wa sp
7.	ri sk	7.	cla p
8.	bas s	8.	gra sp

3 Write the letters and say the word.

sk	sk
a sk	hu sk
ma sk	tu sk
ta sk	**sp**
de sk	ga sp
ri sk	cla sp
whi sk	gra sp
bri sk	cri sp
du sk	

4 Read the words.

desk	ask
husk	task
tusk	
dusk	crisp
risk	gasp
brisk	grasp
whisk	clasp
mask	

5 Write the word you hear.

1.	risk	9.	whisk
2.	ask	10.	crisp
3.	tusk	11.	mask
4.	clasp	12.	brisk
5.	desk	13.	grasp
6.	husk	14.	dusk
7.	task		
8.	gasp		

6 Read the sentences.

New word: boy **Review words:** corn, basket

1. The farmer worked until dusk.
2. Tom asked if there was a big risk.
3. The boys and girls sit at their desks.
4. The cab whisked him off to his office.
5. This is a list of tasks for you to do.
6. My little boy has a funny mask.
7. I was gasping after I ran up the steps.
8. I step out into the crisp, brisk wind.
9. Her task was to cut the grass.
10. Put the corn husks into the basket.
11. You take a risk when you bet money.
12. That boy put on his catcher's mask.
13. This bread has a crisp crust.
14. She grasped my hand and clasped it.
15. Ed asks if he can work at her desk.
16. The pig has two big tusks.

Practice 39: *-lt* **and** *-ld*

Student's page 45

Note: Point out that the *u* is silent in *guilt, built,* and *build.*
Point out the difference in spelling and meaning between *build* and *built.*

1

-lt

bell

belt

-ld

well

weld

2 What does the word end with?

l t lt

1. bel l
2. co lt
3. til l
4. bi t
5. me lt
6. bow l
7. wi lt
8. to t

l d ld

1. we ld
2. fee l
3. hea d
4. mil l
5. mi ld
6. toa d
7. bil l
8. go ld

3 Write the letters and say the word.

lt

be lt
fe lt
me lt
bui lt
gui lt
qui lt
ti lt
wi lt

ld

he ld
we ld
bui ld

4 Read the words.

tilt
built
wilt
quilt
guilt
melt
belt
felt

build
weld
held

5 Write the word you hear.

1. wilt
2. felt
3. held
4. built
5. tilt
6. belt
7. quilt
8. weld
9. guilt
10. melt
11. build

6 Read the sentences. **New words:** over, together **Review word:** butter

1. Grandmother is making a quilt.
2. The belt held up his pants.
3. Melt the fat in the pan.
4. Dad built a desk. It held together.
5. The robber cannot get rid of his guilt.
6. My plant is wilting.
7. We worked together to build the school.
8. When he tilted it back, it fell over.
9. Andy welds two things together.
10. Dan plans to build six buildings.
11. The belt felt good when I put it on.
12. Put the quilt over the bed.
13. Mom held her baby. The baby felt wet.
14. They built a bridge over the river.
15. She felt guilt over what happened.
16. Put the melted butter on the corn.

Practice 40: *-lk, -lp, -lf,* **and** *-lm*
Student's page 46

Note: Point out that *self* can be used alone or in compound words like *herself, himself, myself, yourself,* and *itself.*

1

-lk	**-lf**
mill	shell
milk	shelf

-lp	**-lm**
hell	fill
help	film

2 What does the word end with?

l k lk

1. bil l
2. e lk
3. sic k
4. mi lk
5. buc k
6. wel l
7. su lk
8. hul l

l f lf

1. i f
2. go lf
3. woo l
4. e lf
5. sel l
6. snif f
7. gul l
8. she lf

3 Write the letters and say the word.

lk

e lk
mi lk
si lk

lp

sca lp
he lp
ye lp
gu lp

lf

e lf
se lf
she lf
go lf
gu lf

lm

e lm
fi lm

4 Read the words.

silk	golf
milk	self
elk	shelf
	elf
help	gulf
yelp	
gulp	film
scalp	elm

5 Write the word you hear.

1. help
2. gulf
3. film
4. silk
5. elf
6. gulp
7. shelf
8. milk
9. elm
10. scalp
11. golf
12. yelp
13. self
14. elk

6 Read the sentences.

1. I am making a silk dress for myself.
2. The ship headed into the gulf.
3. I take colored pictures with this film.
4. Pam gulped down a glass of milk.
5. Stan plays golf by himself.
6. We helped Dad cut down the big elm.
7. Scott will put up the shelf himself.
8. The baby wants to do things for herself.
9. My uncle is in the Elks Club.
10. Frank helps himself to some milk.
11. The little elf had fun playing tricks.
12. The silk thread is on the top shelf.
13. She helped me when I hurt myself.
14. The class is watching a good film.
15. The pup yelps when it is hurt.
16. This hat makes my scalp itch!

Practice 41: *-ft*

Student's page 47

1

-ft

rat
raft

sit
sift

2

What does the word end with?

f t ft

1. deaf
2. raft
3. sit
4. theft
5. cat
6. of
7. lift
8. half
9. let
10. shift
11. at
12. clef
13. gift
14. sought
15. draft
16. puff

3

Write the letters and say the word.

ft	ft
raft	sift
shaft	shift
craft	thrift
draft	drift
left	swift
theft	
gift	
lift	

4

Read the words.

sift	raft
drift	shaft
shift	draft
swift	theft
thrift	left
gift	
lift	
craft	

5

Write the word you hear.

1. gift
2. craft
3. drift
4. swift
5. left
6. raft
7. sift
8. thrift
9. draft
10. shift
11. theft
12. lift
13. shaft

6

Read the sentences. **Review word:** after

1. The raft drifted down the river.
2. Sift it to get the lumps out.
3. That draft is giving me a chill.
4. Kim cannot lift her arm.
5. I stress thrift. I do not spend much.
6. I had no money left to pay for the gift.
7. That man is wanted for car theft.
8. We work the last shift at the factory.
9. We asked him for a lift into the city.
10. After one, I left for my crafts class.
11. My aunt works with gifted children.
12. Jack drifted from one job to another.
13. Jill's car has a stick shift.
14. Ned is a swift runner.
15. He tripped and fell down the dark shaft.
16. Ron is skilled in his craft.

Practice 42: *-pt, -ct,* **and** *-xt*

Student's page 48

1

-pt
wet
wept

-ct
fat
fact

-xt
net
next

2 What does the word end with?

p t pt c t ct

1.	wra p	1.	ele ct
2.	ke pt	2.	die t
3.	swea t	3.	rea ct
4.	fli p	4.	basi c
5.	we pt	5.	pilo t
6.	cro p	6.	atti c
7.	a t	7.	dedu ct
8.	scri pt	8.	magi c

3 Write the letters and say the word.

pt	ct
a pt	a ct
ke pt	fa ct
we pt	stri ct
cre pt	**xt**
sle pt	ne xt
swe pt	te xt
scri pt	

4 Read the words.

crept	fact
wept	act
slept	strict
kept	
swept	text
script	next
apt	

5 Write the word you hear.

1. swept
2. act
3. script
4. wept
5. text
6. apt
7. fact
8. slept
9. next
10. kept
11. strict
12. crept

6 Read the sentences. **New words:** study, adopt, expect **Review words:** factory, doctor

1. The judge will study the facts.
2. We kept expecting something to happen.
3. We want to adopt our next kid.
4. Dad acted fast. He swept up the glass.
5. The doctor has not slept much for days.
6. The crab crept over the sand.
7. I expect Ed will act in our next play. He is studying the script for it.
8. We expect to adopt her plan.
9. This is the next text we will study.
10. Pam felt so sad that she wept.
11. The baby crept into the kitchen.
12. He is apt to be strict if they act up.
13. The pup slept next to my bed.
14. This text gives facts on adopted kids.
15. John kept his job at the factory.

Practice 43: Review of Other Ending Blends: ***-mp, -st, -sk, -sp, -lk, -lf, -lm, -lp, -ct, -pt, -xt***

Student's page 49

Note: For this review, follow procedure on page 43, for Review of Beginning Blends.

1 Look at the picture and say the word. Then write the letters of the ending blend you hear.

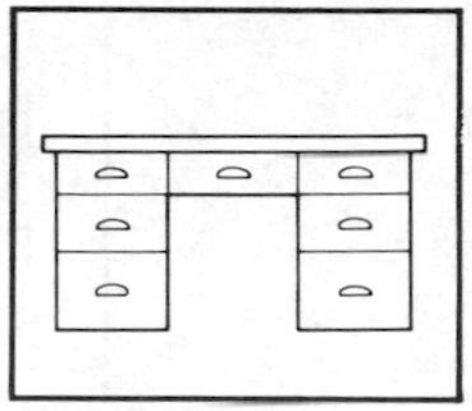

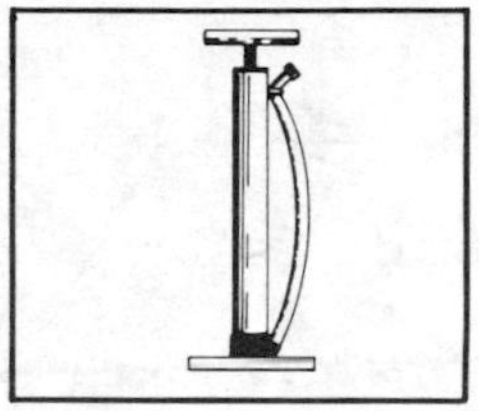

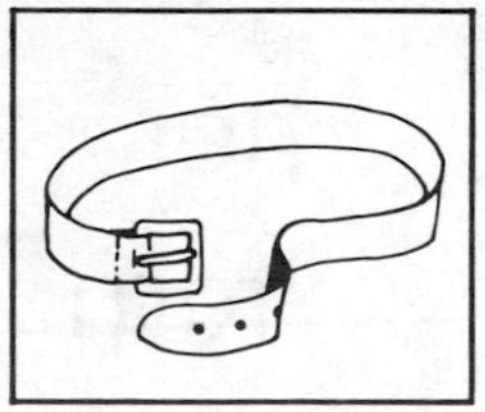

mi lk **de** sk **gi** ft **pu** mp **ve** st **be** lt

2 Circle all the words that are the same as the first one.

mask	mash	(mask)	ask	mast	mash	smack	(mask)
left	lift	felt	(left)	let	(left)	slept	(left)
past	(past)	pat	(past)	pest	pact	(past)	spat
belt	bet	(belt)	bell	built	pelt	(belt)	(belt)

3 Draw a line from each beginning to an ending blend to make a word.

mi	xt
fa	ft
ne	ct
dra	lk

tu	sp
cri	sk
sta	pt
we	mp

4 Use these words to fill in the blanks:

shelf held film help list guilt west risks

1. The car left the camp, heading west on the ramp.
2. Dust the shelf and put the lamp on it.
3. My guest asked me if I wanted any help.
4. The fact was, he felt no guilt for his acts.
5. The champ kept taking risks.
6. Make a list of the tasks you do best.
7. I held the golf club and lifted it over my head.
8. Andy gasped when he watched the film.

Practice 44: *er*

Student's page 50

Note: Point out the differences in spelling and meaning between the homonyms *herd* and *heard.* The word *fern* is used as both a common and proper noun.

1

er

her

fern

were

jerk

2 Write the letters you hear.

er	re

1. t er m
2. f re t
3. v er b
4. f er n
5. re d
6. d re ss
7. cl er k
8. f re sh

3 Write the letters and say the word.

er	er
h er	f er n
v er b	F er n
h er d	st er n
m er ge	v er se
j er k	n er ve
p er k	s er ve
cl er k	sw er ve
t er m	p er ch

4 Read the words.

term	serve
Fern	nerve
fern	swerve
stern	herd
her	perch
perk	verb
jerk	merge
clerk	verse

5 Write the word you hear.

1. jerk
2. serve
3. fern
4. perch
5. term
6. her
7. nerve
8. perk
9. stern
10. verb
11. merge
12. Fern
13. clerk
14. verse
15. swerve
16. herd

6 Read the sentences.

Review words: were, heard, person

1. Fern pays the clerk in the gift shop.
2. I heard him sing the last verse.
3. Make a list of the helping verbs.
4. They serve fresh perch for lunch.
5. Dan is a very strict and stern person.
6. The van stopped with a jerk.
7. I have just one term paper to write.
8. Pam likes ferns best of any plants.
9. The cars merge when they get off the ramp.
10. A hot drink will perk you up.
11. We heard her yelling at the clerk.
    She has a lot of nerve!
12. The car had to swerve to miss the pup.
13. The bird is resting on the perch.
14. Don will serve two terms in office.
15. We were herding the pigs into the pen.

Vowels + *r*

The next nine practices cover the most common sounds of the *r*-controlled vowels *er, ir, ur, ar,* and *or.* The procedure is the same as for the blends practices except for parts 1 and 2.

1

The first part of each practice gives words that have the *r*-controlled vowel sound S. is studying. Follow this procedure, as with *er*:

T. says: When you have an *r* after any of the vowels, it usually changes the sound of the vowel. The vowel doesn't have a regular short sound.
E-r sounds like /er/ not /ehr/.
What does *e-r* sound like? [/er/] Good.
Here are some words that have the *e-r* sound /er/.

Go over each word, helping S. if he has trouble. Some words may be new to him.

As you do part 1 for the first three practices, remind S.:

T. says: *E-r, i-r,* and *u-r* all make the same sound. They sound like /er/.
You will have to remember whether the /er/ sound in words is spelled with *e-r, i-r,* or *u-r,* because you can't tell how the word is spelled by the sound of it.

Be sure S. pronounces the *ar* sound /ar/ correctly. Be sure S. distinguishes it from the /ur/ sound. See page 75 for a discussion of the *or* sound.

2

Write the letters you hear

This exercise helps S. distinguish between the *vowel-r* combination he is studying, and the reverse, the *r-vowel* combination. Follow this procedure:

T. says: You have been studying the *e-r* sound /er/.
It is easy to confuse the *e-r* sound /ur/ with the *r-e* sound /re/ in words, especially when you are spelling them.
This exercise will help you tell the difference.
I will read some words.
If it sounds like the word has the *e-r* sound /er/, write *e-r* in the blank.
If it sounds like the word has the *r-e* sound /re/, write *r-e* in the blank.
Ready? *Term. Term.*

Read each word slowly and distinctly, at least twice. If S. repeats the words after you, make sure he pronounces each one correctly. As he does the exercise, S. might first see if he can recognize the *vowel-r* sound he has been studying. If S. has trouble with a word, you might contrast the word with the word as it would be with the reverse sound (even if that word is a nonsense word). If S. has much difficulty with this part, he may need more exercises like this one to practice.

3

Write the letters and say the word

In this part, S. will be blending the *r*-controlled vowel with consonants and consonant digraphs at the beginning and ending to make words. The words are grouped together by ending sounds.

T. says: What does *e-r* sound like? (Point to *er* at top of column.) [S: /er/]
Good. You can make new words that have the /er/ sound in them.

(Point to *h.*) *H* sounds like /h/. Say /h/. [S: /h/]
If I write *e-r* after *h* (write the letters in), I have the sounds /h/ and /er/. Say those sounds as I point to them.
(Point to *h.*) [S: /h/] (Point to *er*) [S: /er/] Good.
Can you blend those sounds together into a word?
(Help S. if he has trouble.) [S: her] Right.

(Point to *v.*) *V* sounds like /v/. Say /v/. [S: /v/]
And *b* sounds like /b/. Say /b/. [S: /b/] Good.
If I have *v* and then *e-r* (write letters in), and then *b,* I have the sounds /v/ and /er/ and /b/. Say those sounds as I point to them.
(Point to *v*) [S: /v/] (Point to *er*) [S: /er/] (Point to *b*) [S: /b/]
Good. Can you blend those sounds together into a word?
(Help S. if he has trouble.) [S: verb] Right.

Now let's go through the rest of the words.
All the words have the sound /er/, spelled with *e-r.*
You write the letters and read the words.

For the rest of the practice, follow the same procedure as for the other blends practices.

Practice 45: *ir*

Student's page 51

1

ir

bird

girl

skirt

2 Write the letters you hear.

ir ri

1. t ri m
2. d ir t
3. b ir ch
4. c ri b
5. f ir st
6. g ri ll
7. t ri p
8. f ir m

3 Write the letters and say the word.

ir	ir
f ir	ch ir p
s ir	d ir t
st ir	sh ir t
th ir d	squ ir t
wh ir l	b ir ch
tw ir l	b ir th
f ir m	f ir st
squ ir m	th ir st

4 Read the words.

firm	sir
squirm	stir
shirt	fir
dirt	birth
squirt	thirst
twirl	first
whirl	third
chirp	birch

5 Write the word you hear.

1. shirt
2. twirl
3. fir
4. birch
5. chirp
6. firm
7. squirt
8. thirst
9. sir
10. birth
11. whirl
12. squirm
13. third
14. dirt
15. first
16. stir

6 Read the sentences. **New word:** tree **Review words:** bird, girl, skirt

1. Stir in the eggs first, then the nuts.
2. I got dirt on my shirt and my skirt.
3. We planted birch trees and fir trees.
4. I was thrilled after my son's birth!
5. Dad is firm when he says no.
6. The bird sits in the tree, chirping.
7. You will be first, and I will be third.
8. Pat whirls and twirls when she dances.
9. The little girl sat and squirmed.
10. This drink will quench your thirst.
11. Stir it until it gets firm.
12. The pup got mud and dirt on Ed's shirt.
13. Ed says "Yes, sir" to his father.
14. She is giving birth to her third baby.
15. Fern has on a pink skirt.
16. He squirts water on the thirsty plants.

Practice 46: ***ur***

Student's page 52

Note: Point out that *purr* is spelled with two *r's,* but *fur* with only one.

1

ur

hurt

burn

nurse

2

Write the letters you hear.

ur ru

1. c ur l
2. d ru g
3. b ur p
4. t ur n
5. g ru ff
6. c ru sh
7. c ur b
8. d ru m

3

Write the letters and say the word.

ur	ur
f ur	ch ur n
p ur r	b ur p
bl ur	c ur se
c ur b	n ur se
s ur f	p ur se
ur ge	c ur ve
c ur l	ch ur ch
t ur n	b ur st

4

Read the words.

curl	curb
churn	purr
turn	fur
purse	blur
curse	church
nurse	burst
surf	curve
urge	burp

5

Write the word you hear.

1. nurse
2. purr
3. surf
4. burp
5. urge
6. curb
7. curse
8. churn
9. fur
10. burst
11. curve
12. purse
13. church
14. turn
15. blur
16. curl

6

Read the sentences. **New word:** wife **Review words:** hurt, burn, hurry, curtains, cover

1. My cat purrs when I rub her fur.
2. The car turns and stops at the curb.
3. A man grabbed my purse and hurried off.
4. One person is hurt. His hand is burned.
   A nurse covers the burns on his hand.
5. We sit in the sand and watch the surf.
6. Ted's wife urges him to go to church.
7. She fills up her purse. It is bursting!
8. The farmer's wife churns the butter.
9. Fran is curling her hair.
10. Bill burst into the church office.
11. Jim cursed when he hurt his finger.
12. Hurry up and put up the curtains!
13. My wife is burping our baby.
14. The nurses take turns working.
15. The car went fast on the curve.

Practice 47-A: *ar*

Student's page 53

Note: The word *mark* is used as both a common and proper noun.

1

ar

car

barn

mark

park

2 Write the letters you hear.

ra ar

1. d ar k
2. g ra b
3. b ar n
4. ra t
5. d ra g
6. sh ar p
7. c ra sh
8. p ar k

3 Write the letters and say the word.

ar	ar
b ar	b ar k
c ar	d ar k
f ar	l ar k
j ar	m ar k
t ar	M ar k
sc ar	p ar k
st ar	sh ar k
y ar n	sp ar k

4 Read the words.

park	yarn
Mark	far
bark	tar
shark	car
dark	jar
spark	star
mark	bar
lark	scar

5 Write the word you hear.

1. lark
2. tar
3. dark
4. bar
5. shark
6. jar
7. scar
8. mark
9. yarn
10. far
11. spark
12. car
13. star
14. bark
15. Mark
16. park

6 Read the sentences.

Review words: barn, large, market

1. Get a jar of jelly at the market.
2. The park is not far from the school.
3. Fern gets good marks in her math class.
4. When it is dark, we look at the stars.
5. The pup is barking. He is not far off.
6. I am making a hat out of dark red yarn.
7. Ted put a bar under the box to lift it.
8. Sparks fell from the burning barn.
9. Sharks are very large fish.
10. Kim parked her car next to the barn.
11. The street is covered with black tar.
12. Mark had lunch at the snack bar.
13. He has a large scar on his leg.
14. A lark is singing in the park.
15. That tree has a thick bark.
16. We cannot go very far in this car.

Practice 47-B: ***ar***

Student's page 54

Note: Point out that *guard* is spelled with a *u*, although *garden* is not.
Point out the compound words in sentences 1 (birthday) and 2 (barnyard).

1

ar

arm

farm

large

2

Write the letters you hear.

ar ra

1. c ar d
2. b ra n
3. ra sh
4. ar m
5. sc ar f
6. b ra g
7. f ar m
8. g ra ss

3

Write the letters and say the word.

ar	ar
c ar d	h ar m
gu ar d	ch ar m
h ar d	b ar ge
l ar d	l ar ge
y ar d	M ar ge
sc ar f	ch ar ge
C ar l	h ar p
sn ar l	sh ar p

4

Read the words.

sharp	hard
harp	yard
large	guard
charge	lard
barge	card
Marge	charm
snarl	harm
Carl	scarf

5

Write the word you hear.

1. yard
2. harp
3. barge
4. card
5. Marge
6. harm
7. snarl
8. lard
9. scarf
10. charge
11. Carl
12. sharp
13. guard
14. large
15. hard
16. charm

6

Read the sentences.

Review words: arm, farm, farmer, garden

1. Marge is sending Carl a birthday card.
2. We have a large barnyard on our farm.
3. The pup snarls at me. Will it harm me?
4. My wife plants a garden in the yard.
5. Large barges carry goods up the river.
6. Marge has her good luck charm with her.
7. The farmer works hard on his farm.
8. The bark on that tree is hard.
9. It has a sharp edge. It cuts well.
10. Carl hands the clerk his charge card.
11. Lard is the fat that comes from pigs.
12. A large yarn scarf covers her head.
13. Marge can play the harp.
14. Our garden is six yards by ten yards.
15. Armed guards kept him from harm.
16. There is no charge for parking there.

Practice 47-C: ***ar***

Student's page 55

Note: The word *march* is used both as a common and proper noun.

1

ar

start

Arthur

march

2 Write the letters you hear.

ar	ra

1. t ra p
2. d ar t
3. c ra b
4. b ar k
5. st ar ch
6. b ra t
7. t ra sh
8. p ar t

3 Write the letters and say the word.

ar	ar
ar t	c ar ve
c ar t	st ar ve
d ar t	h ar sh
p ar t	m ar sh
t ar t	ar ch
ch ar t	m ar ch
sm ar t	M ar ch
st ar t	st ar ch

4 Read the words.

part	marsh
chart	harsh
art	March
start	arch
cart	starch
smart	march
dart	carve
tart	starve

5 Write the word you hear.

1. march
2. dart
3. chart
4. carve
5. start
6. arch
7. marsh
8. art
9. starch
10. cart
11. harsh
12. tart
13. starve
14. part
15. March
16. smart

6 Read the sentences: **New words:** love, army, Barb **Review words:** Arthur, Indian

1. Put a jar of nuts in the shopping cart.
2. The army started marching up the hill.
3. Mom puts starch in Dad's shirts.
4. Arthur loves his arts and crafts class.
5. Barb is making little apple tarts.
6. Water covers a large part of the marsh.
7. Dad started to carve the hen.
8. In March, the army ended the draft.
9. My sister Barb loves to play darts.
10. Arthur is smart. He makes good marks.
11. What part do you act in the play?
12. Her red, chapped hands felt harsh.
13. The head of the army is studying charts.
14. My cat arched her back and hissed.
15. I am starved! When do we have lunch?
16. Barb loves to study Indian art.

The Sound *or* in Practices 48-A and 48-B

The *or* practices follow exactly the same procedure as the previous *vowel-r* practices. There is just one thing to keep in mind about the *or* sound /or/, however. The sound is actually a *long* vowel sound, or close to it. The /or/ sound is included here so that S. can contrast it with the other *r*-controlled vowels, and practice blending the sound with consonant sounds that come before it and after it. You may want to call S.'s attention to this different sound. Make sure S. can recognize the /or/ sound and pronounce it correctly.

Although practices 48-A and 48-B have many *or* words, those practices do not include words which are spelled with *ore* or *oar. Ore* and *oar* words will be covered in the next workbook in this series, *Focus on Phonics-3.* They are saved for that workbook because they illustrate the long vowel rules well. You might want to explain to S. why he will study these words later if he asks about them. Or if S. has already studied long vowels, and you want to present these words to him, there is a brief list below for your reference. Also included in the list are words having the /or/ sound spelled with *oor* and *our:*

/or/ spelled *ore*: bore, core, more, pore, sore, tore, wore, shore, chore, score, snore, spore, store, swore.

/or/ spelled *oar*: oar, soar, roar, board, hoard.

/or/ spelled *oor*: door, floor.

/or/ spelled *our*: four, pour, mourn, court, course.

Practice 48-A: *or*

Student's page 56

1

or

or

for

corn

2 Write the letters you hear.

or ro

1. b or n
2. t ro t
3. f or k
4. p ro p
5. c or d
6. b ro th
7. ro b
8. t or n

3 Write the letters and say the word.

or	or
or	b or n
c or d	c or n
F or d	h or n
l or d	t or n
c or k	w or n
f or k	th or n
p or k	sc or n
st or k	sw or n

4 Read the words.

torn	or
corn	fork
sworn	stork
thorn	cork
horn	pork
scorn	Ford
worn	cord
born	lord

5 Write the word you hear.

1. fork
2. worn
3. cord
4. born
5. scorn
6. or
7. Ford
8. stork
9. corn
10. thorn
11. pork
12. lord
13. horn
14. cork
15. sworn
16. torn

6 Read the sentences.

New words: morning, new **Review word:** York

1. My new Ford has a good horn!
2. The plant is covered with sharp thorns.
3. We were born in New York City.
4. Give me a fork. I will carve this pork.
5. She was sworn into office this morning.
6. Ed trips over the cord of the TV set.
7. Jack has no job, but do not scorn him.
8. He has not worn that shirt. It is torn.
9. Serve corn or bread with the pork.
10. The stork visited them this morning! A new baby was born to them!
11. Barb asks, "Lord God, help us!"
12. Put the dishes and forks in the sink.
13. The farmer picks corn every morning.
14. Mark plays his new horn in the band.
15. Put the cork back in to stop it up.

Practice 48-B: *or*

Student's page 57

Note: Point out the differences between *forth* and its homonym *fourth.*

1

or

or

for

short

2

Write the letters you hear.

or	ro

1. c ro p
2. f or m
3. p or t
4. ro t
5. t or ch
6. d ro p
7. f or t
8. p ro m

3

Write the letters and say the word.

or	or
f or t	f or ce
p or t	h or se
s or t	p or ch
sh or t	t or ch
sp or t	sc or ch
sn or t	f or th
f or m	n or th
st or m	f or ge

4

Read the words.

torch	forge
porch	force
scorch	sort
storm	port
form	short
horse	snort
north	fort
forth	sport

5

Write the word you hear.

1. short
2. north
3. force
4. storm
5. torch
6. port
7. forge
8. snort
9. fort
10. horse
11. sport
12. scorch
13. forth
14. sort
15. porch
16. form

6

Read the sentences.

1. Marge is sitting out on the porch.
2. I fill out the short form to pay taxes.
   I have to force myself to do it.
3. The army marched north to the fort.
4. What sort of sports do you like best?
5. The horse lifted his head and snorted.
6. Carl forged my name to a check.
7. When it got dark, Ed lit a torch.
8. There is a bad storm north of us.
9. I scorched the shirt. It is burned.
10. Bill is the best cop on the force.
11. I am short, but I play in many sports.
12. The ship is coming into port.
13. We are forming a sports club.
14. The women are sorting the letters.
15. The horse went forth into the storm.

Practice 49: Review of Vowels + *r*: *er, ir, ur, ar, or*

Student's page 58

1 Look at the picture and say the word. Then write the letters for the sounds you hear.

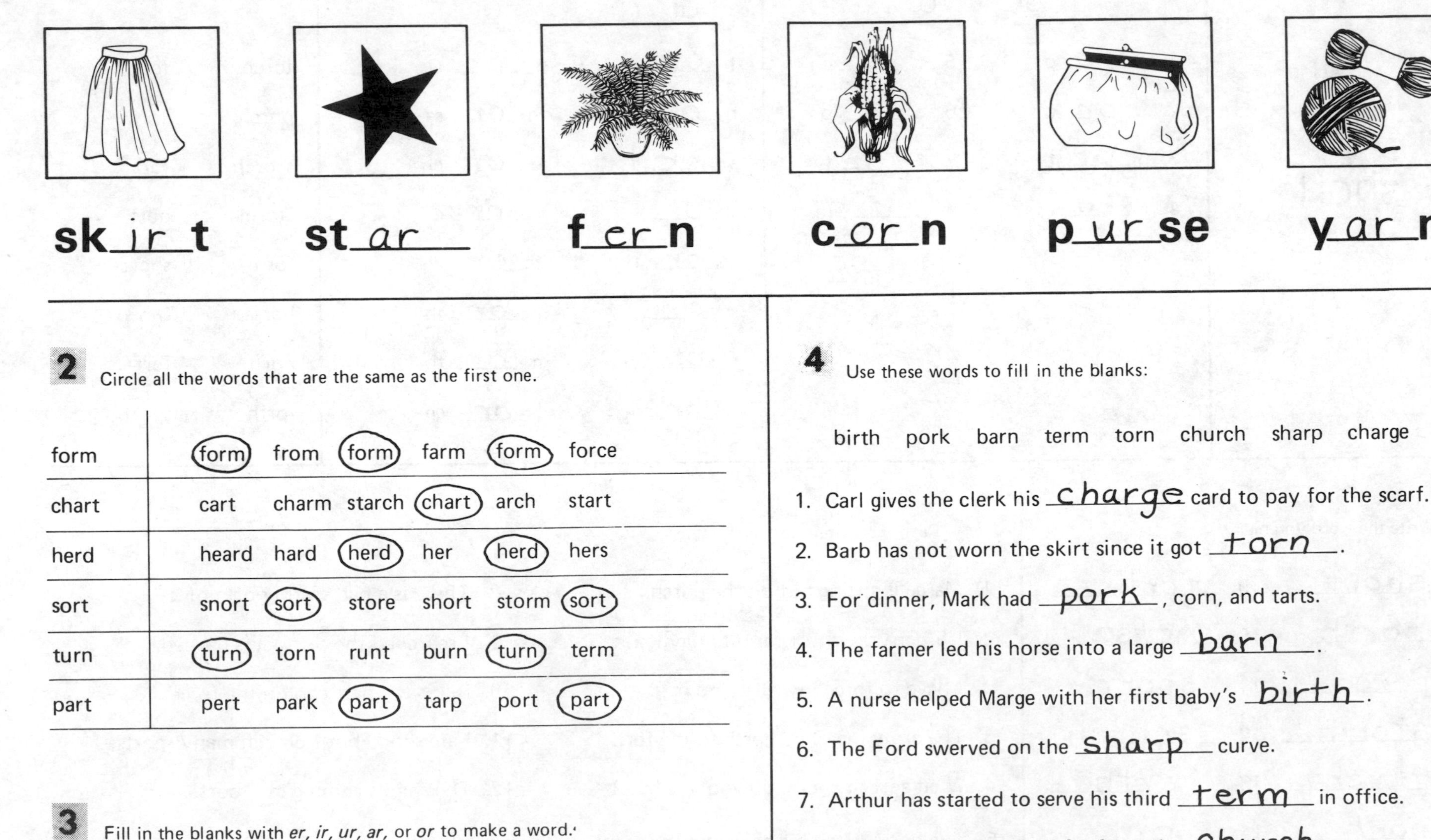

sk ir **t** **st** ar **f** er **n** **c** or **n** **p** ur **se** **y** ar **n**

2 Circle all the words that are the same as the first one.

form	(form) from (form) farm (form) force
chart	cart charm starch (chart) arch start
herd	heard hard (herd) her (herd) hers
sort	snort (sort) store short storm (sort)
turn	(turn) torn runt burn (turn) term
part	pert park (part) tarp port (part)

3 Fill in the blanks with *er, ir, ur, ar,* or *or* to make a word.

1. ch ar m
2. ur ge
3. sn or t
4. j er k
5. b ur p
6. c or n
7. y ar d
8. tw ir l
9. t er m

4 Use these words to fill in the blanks:

birth pork barn term torn church sharp charge

1. Carl gives the clerk his charge card to pay for the scarf.
2. Barb has not worn the skirt since it got torn.
3. For dinner, Mark had pork, corn, and tarts.
4. The farmer led his horse into a large barn.
5. A nurse helped Marge with her first baby's birth.
6. The Ford swerved on the sharp curve.
7. Arthur has started to serve his third term in office.
8. Fern parked her car not far from the church.

Practice 49: Review of Vowels + *r*

T. says: In this practice, you will review the *r* combinations you have studied: *e-r, i-r, u-r, a-r,* and *o-r.*

1

T. says: Look at the picture and say the word.
Then fill in the letters that make the sound you hear.

Be sure S. pronounces each word correctly. S. fills in the *r* combination that makes the sounds he hears. Since *er, ir,* and *ur* all sound alike, S. must remember from studying those three practices which combination goes with which word.

2

T. says: Circle all the words that are the same as the first.
Work from left to right.

This is primarily a *visual* discrimination exercise. It is useful for giving evidence of visual problems like poor vision, directional problems, and reversals of letters and words. It is very important for you to note the kinds of errors S. makes. Some of the incorrect words are new to S., but they *look* like the word to be circled. In some cases, an incorrect word is the same as the circled word except for the vowel. If S. makes an error by circling these words, he is probably not noticing the vowels or the *r* combinations in words. If S. makes many mistakes in this visual discrimination exercise (three or more), you should check further for visual problems.

T. says: The words listed below have some letters missing.
You have had these words before.
You must fill in *e-r, i-r, u-r, a-r,* or *o-r* in each one to make a word.
Then read the word.

For some words, S. may have to try the *r* combinations one by one to see which one fits (only one is possible). S. should recognize a word after he fills in the right combination, since he has studied the words before. He must use his memory as well as his knowledge of sounds, since *er, ir,* and *ur* all sound alike.

4

T. says: Here are eight words that you have seen before. (Point to words.)
They have the *r* combinations that you are reviewing.
Read the words. (Go over the words and their meanings with S.)
Now you will use those eight words in sentences.
Read each sentence and fill in the word that makes sense.
Use each word just once.

Practice 50: *ear* **and** *wor*

Student's page 59

1

ear = /er/

heard

learn

wor = /wer/

word

work

2

Circle the word you hear.

1. word (cord)
2. (heard) hard
3. (work) fork
4. yearn (yarn)
5. earth (art)
6. (worm) form
7. (worst) was
8. worth (north)

3

Write the letters and say the word.

ear	wor
h ear d	wor d
Ear l	wor k
p ear l	wor m
ear n	wor se
l ear n	wor st
y ear n	wor th
s ear ch	wor ld
ear th	

4

Read the words.

learn	worm
earn	worth
yearn	worse
pearl	worst
Earl	word
earth	world
search	work
heard	

5

Write the word you hear.

1. pearl
2. work
3. learn
4. worth
5. Earl
6. worse
7. yearn
8. worm
9. search
10. world
11. heard
12. worst
13. earth
14. word
15. earn

6

Read the sentences.

New words: worry, about

1. Earl works to earn money.
2. That string of pearls is worth a lot.
3. I yearn to visit the rest of the world.
4. Earl is learning to spell many words.
5. Ned is searching for worms for fishing.
6. Worrying about it just makes it worse.
7. The cops search for the missing pearls.
8. This car is the worst! It never works!
9. I have not heard a word he said.
10. Do not worry! The worst is over!
11. The worms are digging in the earth.
12. She earns about fifty dollars a day.
13. We heard about Earl. He is very sick.
    We worry that he will get worse.
14. We learned about the earth's crust.
15. This work is not worth doing.

Practice 50: *ear* and *wor*

This practice introduces some words that have the sound /er/ spelled *e-a-r* and the sound /wer/ spelled *w-o-r*.

T. says: By now you've learned many words that have the /er/ sound.
Those words were spelled with *e-r, i-r,* or *u-r.*
In this practice, you will learn some other words that have /er/ sounds.

1

T. says: The words in the first group are spelled with *e-a-r* plus another consonant. (Point to *heard* at the top of the page.)
But you will read them as if they had no *a,* as if they were spelled with *e-r,* instead of *e-a-r.*
They have the *e-r* sound /er/ in them.
You have seen this word before. (Point to *heard* again.)
What is it? [S: heard] Good.
In *heard,* the *e-a-r* sounds like /er/.
What do you think this word is? (Point to the second word.)
[S: learn] Good. (Help S. sound out the word if he needs help.)
Can you see that the *e-a-r* makes the /er/ sound in *learn*?

2

T. says: In the words you've studied with *o-r,* the *o-r* makes the sound /or/.
But that's not true for most words spelled *w-o-r.* (Point to *wor.*)
In these words, the *w-o-r* sounds like this: /wer/.
Say the sound /wer/. [/wer/] Right.
The two words listed below *wor* are words you've seen before.
What is this word? (Point to *word.*) [S: word] Good.
What is this word? (Point to *work.*) [S: work] Right.
Can you hear that in both *word* and *work,* the *w-o-r* sounds like /wer/?
Now let's look at some more *e-a-r* and *w-o-r* words.

3

T. says: What does *e-a-r* sound like when it is followed by another consonant?
[S: /er/] Good.
You can make new words that have the /er/ sound in them.
They are spelled with *e-a-r.* (Point to *ear* at the top of the first column.)
If I have *h* and then *e-a-r* (write these letters in), and then *d,*
I have the sounds /h/, /er/, /d/.
Say those sounds as I point to the letters.
(Point to *h.*) [S: /h/] (Point to *e-a-r.*) [S: /er/] (Point to *d.*) [S: /d/]
Now blend those sounds together into a word. [S: heard] Good.
(Help S. if he has trouble.)

T. says: The next word is a name. *E-a-r* sounds like /er/. (Point to the letters that are written in.)
And *l* sounds like /l/. (Point to *l.*)
Say those sounds as I point to them.
(Point to *Ear.*) [S: /er/] (Point to *l.*) [S: /l/]
Can you blend those sounds together into a word?
[S: Earl] Good. (Help S. if he has trouble.)
Now let's go through the rest of the words in this column.
All the words have the sound /er/ spelled with *e-a-r.*
You write the letters and read the words.

When S. has finished the first column, proceed to the second.

T. says: What does *w-o-r* sound like when it is followed by another consonant?
[S: /wer/] Good.
You can make new words that have the /wer/ sound in them.
They all start with *w-o-r.*
If I write *w-o-r* before *d* (write these letters in), I have the sounds /wer/ and /d/.
Say those sounds as I point to the letters.
(Point to *w-o-r.*) [S: /wer/] (Point to *d.*) [S: /d/] Good.
Now blend those sounds together into a word. [S: word] Good.
(Help S. if he has trouble.)

Now let's go through the rest of the words.
All the words have the sound /wer/ spelled with *w-o-r.*
You write the letters and read the words.

Help S. with the rest of the words. Two of them, *worst* and *world,* have consonant blends after *wor.*

For the rest of the practice, follow the same procedure as for the other *vowel-r* practices, or blends practices.

Practice 51: Compound Words

Student's page 60

1 Look at these compound words:

sunlamp	sun	lamp	fingerprint	finger	print	slingshot	sling	shot
hairbrush	hair	brush	inchworm	inch	worm	quicksand	quick	sand

2 Put the two words together to make a compound word. Read the word.

hand	stand	handstand	land	mark	landmark	sand	paper	sandpaper
work	bench	workbench	egg	plant	eggplant	out	smart	outsmart
left	over	leftover	her	self	herself	sun	glasses	sunglasses
sports	cast	sportscast	back	track	backtrack	wind	storm	windstorm

3 Find the two smaller words in each compound word. Write them in the blanks. Read the smaller words and the compound word.

riverbank	river	bank	windchill	wind	chill	pitchfork	pitch	fork
stopwatch	stop	watch	grandfather	grand	father	standstill	stand	still
snapshot	snap	shot	cornstarch	corn	starch	yardstick	yard	stick
drumstick	drum	stick	underwater	under	water	blacksmith	black	smith

4 Make compound words. Match each word on the left with a word on the right. Write the compound word in the blank. The first one is done for you.

flash	flashback	stop	street	streetcar	grass	play	plaything	born
witch	witchcraft	mark	crab	crabgrass	mother	milk	milkman	west
short	shortstop	craft	silk	silkworm	car	first	firstborn	man
birth	birthmark	back	step	stepmother	worm	north	northwest	thing

Practice 51: Compound words

Before discussing compound words, introduce S. to the idea of syllables.

T. says: You will soon find yourself reading bigger words.
The bigger words have two or more parts.
We call the parts *syllables.*
The syllables are the beats or parts you hear when you say the word.
Let me give you some examples.

These words have only one beat when you say them, even though there are many sounds in the word: (Clap once as you say each word.)
blast drill spin gift pump truck land stop
Each of these words has *one* syllable.
These words have two beats when you say them:
(Clap twice with each word.)
basket kitchen building garden color plenty
Each of these words has *two* syllables.

A word has a syllable *for every vowel sound you hear.*
But if it's hard for you to tell the number of vowel sounds in the word, say the word and listen to the number of beats or parts in it.

When S. understands what syllables are, see whether he can identify the number of syllables in the words he hears.

T. says: Now I will read you some words you've had in your reading.
You listen and tell me how many syllables each word has.
You can say the word after me or clap if you want to.

mask (1)	went (1)
baby (2)	Indian (3)
grandmother (3)	list (1)
stitch (1)	never (1)
ready (2)	twenty (2)
blink (1)	family (3)
market (2)	grip (1)
spell (1)	farmer (2)

If S. makes a mistake, repeat the word slowly and clap as you say it. When S. understands syllables well, go on to compound words.

1

T. says: Now you'll figure out some big words that have two or more syllables.
They are called *compound words.*
Compound words are big words made out of two smaller words.

Look at the compound words at the top of this page. (Point to words.)
Can you see the two smaller words in each of the big words?
The smaller words are written next to the compound words.
In a compound word, the two little words are right together with no space in between them.

Go over the examples of compound words.

T. says: Now look at these words.
Put the two smaller words together to make a compound word.
Write them in the blanks.
Read the smaller words and the compound word.

Check S.'s work as he reads the words. You may want to discuss the meanings of the words.

T. says: Now look at these compound words.
Find the two smaller words in each compound word.
Write them in the blanks.
Read the smaller words and the compound word.

4

T. says: These are words you've read before.
Make a compound word with each of these words (point to the words on the left) by finding another word over here to go with it (point to the words on the right).
Write the compound word in the blank, next to the first word. The first one is done for you.
Then read the compound words you've made.

S. may want to read through the lists of words in each group before starting. Check S.'s work as you have him read the words. You may want to discuss the meanings of the compound words.

After S. finishes all of the exercises, you may have him read through all the compound words and write the number of syllables in each word.

Practice 52: Two-syllable Words

Student's page 61

1 The big words below have been divided into syllables. Using what you have learned about sounding out words, sound out the syllables, and figure out each word.

plastic /**plas** tic/ skillet /**skil** lut/ clever /**clev** er/ intend /in **tend**/

2 Read the word first. Then read the sentence.

1. constant /**con** stant/ We cannot stand that constant yelling!
2. product /**prod** uct/ This shop sells a good product for less.
3. clinic /**clin** ic/ This nurse works in a big clinic.
4. credit /**cred** it/ Dad hands the clerk his credit card.
5. intend /in **tend**/ Jan does not intend to marry Frank.
6. skillet /**skil** lut/ Melt the butter in the hot skillet.
7. profit /**prof** ut/ Dan made a profit on the stock market.

3 Read the word. Fill in the blank. Read the sentence.

1. pumpkin /**pump** kin/ Mom is making pumpkin bread.
2. current /**cur** runt/ Yesterday's newspaper is not current.
3. selfish /**self** ish/ Do not be selfish! Give it to me!
4. problem /**prob** lum/ I tell my problem to my best friend.
5. suburb /**sub** urb/ They live in a suburb of a big city.
6. plastic /**plas** tic/ The cups and dishes are plastic.

4 Read the story.

My Aunt Marge runs a factory in the suburbs.
Her factory makes pots, pans, and skillets.
She is working on her current product, a new skillet.
She says, "Ours will be the best product on the market!
We will run constant tests on it to get rid of any problems."
I have to give Aunt Marge a lot of credit.
She is smart and a hard worker.
She does not just make skillets.
She thinks up clever ads to sell them.
As you can guess, my aunt's factory makes a big profit!

5 Fill in each blank with one of these words.

frantic /**fran** tic/
sandwich /**sand** wich/
trumpet /**trum** put/
traffic /**traf** fic/
squirrel /**squir** rul/
gravel /**grav** ul/

1. A cop is stopping the traffic.
2. The squirrel hid some nuts.
3. Mother was frantic with worry.
4. Fran plays a trumpet in the band.
5. Put the sandwich in a plastic bag.
6. The dump truck is carrying gravel.

Practice 52: Two-syllable Words

Note: Put the stress on the **boldface** syllables when you pronounce the words.

1

T. says: You have learned to sound out many words with short vowels and blends.
This practice will help you sound out many big words, too.
Look at the big words below. (Point to the words.)
The syllable that is in *boldface type* is the *stressed* one.
The *stressed* syllable is the one that has the emphasis, or the hardest beat when you say the word.
The syllable that is not in boldface type is the *unstressed* one.
It has less emphasis when you say it.
Using what you have learned about sounding out words, sound out the syllables and figure out each word.

Look at this word. (Point to *plastic.*)
There's a *c* at the end of the word.
At the end of a word, *c* makes the sound /k/.
How would you say the first syllable? [S: /plas/] Good.
And the second syllable? [S: /tic/] Good.
Now put them together. What's the word? [S: plastic] Good.
(Help S. sound out the syllables if necessary.)

(The word *plastic* is used as an example because S. is used to seeing the ending sound /k/ spelled with a *ck* in many one-syllable words. S. should know that the sound /k/ at the end of many two-syllable words is spelled with just a *c.*)

You can see that the first syllable is *stressed.*
It has the hardest beat. It gets the emphasis.
Can you hear how the first syllable is emphasized when you say the word *plastic?* You don't say /plas **tic**/. You say /**plas** tic/.
Can you hear the difference?

Now look at this word. (Point to *skillet.*)
How would you say the first syllable? [S: /skil/] Good.
This syllable is the *stressed* one.
The next syllable is unstressed.
In many unstressed syllables, the vowel is pronounced like a short *u*: /u/.
In this word, the vowel is pronounced like a short *u*: /uh/.
How would you say this syllable? (Point to *let.*) [S: /lut/] Good.
So how do you say the word? [S: skillet] Good.

T. says: Notice that there are two *l*'s in the middle of the word.
When you put the two syllables together and say the word, you say just one /l/ sound.
How do you say this word again? (Point to *skillet.*) [S: skillet]
Good.

(The term for the unstressed vowel sound is *schwa.* It is shown in dictionaries as an upside down *e*. You may want to show S. some examples from dictionaries.)

Continue with part 1, helping S. where necessary.

T. says: Now you will read several other big words.
These words have been divided into syllables.
Sound out the syllables and figure out each word.
Remember that the boldface syllable is the *stressed* one.
Then read the sentence that uses that word.

3

T. says: Here are some more new words.
Read each word and write it in the blank.
Then read the sentence with that word.

4

T. says: Here is a story with many of the new words you've learned in it.
Read the story.

5

T. says: On the left are six more new words.
Figure out those words.
Then use each of those words just once in one of the sentences at the right.

Practice 53-A: CC - *le* Words with a Double Consonant in the Middle

Student's page 62

1 The big words below have been divided into syllables. Using what you have learned about sounding out words, sound out the syllables and figure out the words.

apple /**ap** pul/ little /**lit** tul/ shuffle /**shuf** ful/ tickle /**tic** kul/

2 Read the word first. Then read the sentence.

1. saddle /**sad** dul/ Saddle up the horses.
2. wiggle /**wig** gul/ The baby wiggles its legs.
3. pickle /**pic** kul/ Put some pickles on the bun.
4. kettle /**ket** tul/ Mom is making jelly in a big kettle.
5. puddle /**pud** dul/ John fell in the puddle and got wet.
6. tackle /**tac** kul/ Ed takes his tackle box when he fishes.
7. nibble /**nib** bul/ My son nibbles on the chips.

3 Read the word. Fill in the blank. Read the sentence.

1. bottle /**bot** tul/ A bottle of ink is on his desk.
2. tickle /**tic** kul/ My baby laughs when I tickle her.
3. rattle /**rat** tul/ The baby plays with a rattle.
4. puzzle /**puz** zul/ Did you put the puzzle together?
5. struggle /**strug** gul/ Dan had to struggle to pass the test.
6. settle /**set** tul/ Fred wants to settle in this city.

4 Read the story.

My little son Mark is three.
Yesterday I was tickling him.
He wiggled out of my arms and ran out into the yard.
Then he sat down in a mud puddle!
After lunch, I said, "Settle down with a puzzle."
"No!" Mark said. He did not want any puzzles.
I heard a rattle. Mark was playing with my pans and kettles.
I said "Stop!" and handed him an apple to nibble on.
Next I heard a crash! He had dropped a bottle of pickles.
Living with a boy of three can be a struggle!
But I want another kid just like him!

5 Fill in each blank with one of these *-le* words.

buckle /**buc** kul/
cattle /**cat** tul/
raffle /**raf** ful/
bubble /**bub** bul/
middle /**mid** dul/
ripple /**rip** pul/

1. Give me a pack of bubble gum.
2. I rest in the middle of the day.
3. The river has lots of ripples.
4. Did Stan win a car in the raffle?
5. The belt buckle is made of brass.
6. Ted has a large herd of cattle.

Practice 53-A: CC-*le* Words with a Double Consonant in the Middle

T. says: You have had practice sounding out some compound words and other two-syllable words. In the next two practices, you will learn to read some more two-syllable words.
All these words will have something in common.
They will have two consonants and an *l-e* at the end of the word.
In the first practice, the two consonants will have the same sound.

1

T. says: Look at the words in this part.
They have been divided into syllables. Let's sound them out.
You have seen this word. What is it? (Point to *apple.*)
[S: apple] Good.

Apple is divided into syllables here. (Point to syllables.)
The first syllable, /ap/, is the *stressed* syllable.
Remember, the *stressed* syllable is the one that gets the emphasis when you say the word. It has the hardest beat.
Now, at the end of a word, *l-e* makes the sound /ul/.
Say /ul/. [S: /ul/] Good.
Now, what is the first syllable? (Point to **ap**.) [S: /ap/]

What is the second syllable? (Point to *pul.*) [S: /pul/]
Notice that *apple* has two *p*'s in the middle.
When you put the two syllables together and say the word, you say just one /p/ sound.
How do you say this word again? (Point to *apple.*)
[S: apple] Good.

All the words you will learn in these two practices end with *l-e.*
Remember that at the end of a word, *l-e* makes the sound /ul/.
The syllable before /ul/ is always *stressed.*

Go over the familiar word *little* and the new word *shuffle* the same way. Then explain the word *tickle* this way:

T. says: All of the words in this practice have a double consonant before the *l-e,* except for the words that end *c-k-l-e.*
The letters *c-k* together are like a double consonant.
They make the same sound, /k/.
(Point to **tic.**) How do you say this syllable? [S: /tic/] Good.
You have *l-e* at the end of the word. What does that sound like?
[S: /ul/] Good.
So how do you say the word? [S: tickle] Right.

T. says: Now you will read some other words like those you just learned.
They have been divided into syllables.
Sound out the syllables and figure out each word.
Remember that *l-e* at the end of a word makes the sound /ul/.
Remember that the syllable *before* the *l-e* is the stressed one.
Then read the sentence that uses that word.

3

T. says: Here are some more new words.
Read each word and write it in the blank.
Then read the sentence with that word.

T. says: Here is a story with many of the new words you've learned in it.
Read the story.

5

T. says: On the left are six more new words.
Figure out those words.
Then use each word just once in one of the sentences at the right.
Then read the sentences.

Practice 53-B: CC - *le* Words with Two Different Consonants in the Middle

Student's page 63

1 The big words below have been divided into syllables. Sound out the syllables and figure out the words.

handle /**han** dul/ gamble /**gam** bul/ single /**sing** gul/ ankle /**ang** kul/ whistle /**whis** ul/

2 Read the word first. Then read the sentence.

1. tangle /**tang** gul/ The yarn is tangled up.
2. stumble /**stum** bul/ Dad stumbled over the trash can.
3. sample /**sam** pul/ I will sample the punch.
4. twinkle /**twing** kul/ We look at the stars twinkle.
5. swindle /**swin** dul/ He swindled her out of her money.
6. candle /**can** dul/ It was dark, so I lit a candle.
7. gamble /**gam** bul/ Mark never wins when he gambles.

4 Fill in each blank with one of the *-le* words.

handle /**han** dul/
thimble /**thim** bul/
ankle /**ang** kul/
castle /**cas** ul/
temple /**tem** pul/
single /**sing** gul/
uncle /**ung** kul/

1. The king lives in a castle.
2. They go to church in the temple.
3. Pick it up by the handle.
4. Hank is not married. He is single.
5. Chuck fell and turned his ankle.
6. The thimble is big for my finger.
7. Uncle Bob is Dad's brother.

3 Read the word. Fill in the blank. Read the sentence.

1. simple /**sim** pul/ This math is simple, not hard.
2. jungle /**jung** gul/ The men walked out of the jungle.
3. scramble /**scram** bul/ Scramble the eggs for dinner.
4. bundle /**bun** dul/ Kim carries a bundle under her arm.
5. angle /**ang** gul/ Cut it on an angle.
6. tremble /**trem** bul/ Her hands started to tremble.

5 *r*-C-*le* words. Read the word and the sentence.

1. turtle /**tur** tul/ Barb gets a turtle at the pet shop.
2. marble /**mar** bul/ The children are playing marbles.
3. girdle /**gir** dul They sell girdles at the dress shop.
4. sparkle /**spar** kul/ Your ring sparkles!
5. purple /**pur** pul/ Her skirt is pink and purple.
6. startle /**star** tul/ The telephone ring startled me.

Practice 53-B: CC-*le* Words with Two Different Consonants in the Middle

T. says: In this practice, like the last one, you will sound out more words that end with two consonants and an *l-e.*
But in this practice, there are two different consonants before the *l-e.*
In all of these words, the syllable before the *l-e* is the stressed syllable.

1

T. says: Let's look at the words in this part.
They have been divided into syllables. Let's sound them out.
Here is the first word. (Point to *handle.*)
How would you say the first syllable, *h-a-n*? [S: /han/] Good.
Now here's *d-l-e.*
Remember that *l-e* at the end of a word makes the sound /ul/.
How do you say *d-l-e*? [S: /dul/] Good.
Can you put the syllables together to make a word?
[S: handle] Good.

Help S. if he has trouble. Repeat the process with the next word, *gamble.*

T. says: The next word has an *n-g* in it. (Point to *single.*)
When a word ends with *n-g-l-e,* the *g* has two jobs.
First, it is part of *n-g,* which makes the sound /ng/.
So the first syllable of this word is /sing/.
Then *g* has the sound /g/ in the *g-l-e* syllable.
So, the second syllable is /gul/.
How do you say this syllable? (Point to **sing.**) [S: /sing/]
How do you say this syllable? (Point to /gul/.) [S: /gul/]
Can you put the syllables together to make a word? [S: single]
Good.

The next word ends with *n-k-l-e.* (Point to *ankle.*)
Before *k, n* makes the sound /ng/.
So this syllable (point to **ang**) is pronounced /ang/.

T. says: Say /ang/. [S: /ang/] Good.
The next syllable is *k-l-e.*
How do you say that? [S: /kul/] Good.
Can you put the two syllables together to make a word?
[S: ankle] Right.

Now look at the last word. (Point to *whistle.*)
It ends with *s-t-l-e.* The *t* is silent.
In all words that end *s-t-l-e,* the *t* is silent.
How do you say this syllable? (Point to **whis.**) [S: /whis/] Good.
How do you say this syllable? (Point to *le.*) [S: /ul/] Right.
Can you put the syllables together to make a word?
Remember, the *t* is silent.
[S: whistle] Good.

2

T. says: Now you will read some more words like those you just learned.
They have been divided into syllables.
Sound out the syllables and figure out each word.
Remember that the syllable before the *l-e* is the stressed one.
Then read the sentence that uses that word.

3

T. says: Here are some new words.
Read each word and write it in the blank.
Then read the sentence that uses that word.

4

T. says: On the left are seven more words.
Figure out those words.
Then use each word just once in one of the sentences at the right.

5

T. says: These words have an *r* before the consonant-*l-e.*
Remember that *a-r* sounds like /ar/.
Remember that *e-r, i-r,* and *u-r* all sound like /er/.
After you figure out each word, read the sentence that uses that word.

Practice 54: Story

Student's page 64

Shopping at the Department Store

New words: Carter, apartment, department, store, handle

Marge Carter lives in a large apartment.
She says, "This is the day to go shopping.
I will go to the new department store I have heard about.
A person can get many things in a large department store."

Marge hurries out of the apartment.
She starts her car and heads for the department store.
The department store is on North First Street.
It is not far from the apartment.
She turns her car into the large parking lot and parks.

Marge gets a cart and starts shopping.
First Marge looks at a box of gift cards. It is marked $2.00.
She puts the cards in her cart.
Then she picks up some brushes.
"My son Carl will want some brushes for his art class," she says.

The third thing she picks up is a scarf.
The scarf is made of red yarn.
"My girl Barb will like this scarf," she says.

Then Marge looks at some shirts.
She thinks, "Mark wants a new sports shirt. His red one is torn."
She puts a shirt in the cart.

Next she picks out some kitchen curtains.
And she picks up some jars for canning.
Last she picks up some ferns and other plants for the apartment.

The clerk asks Marge, "Will this be cash or charge?"

Marge says, "I am short of cash."
She takes a charge card out of her purse and hands it to the clerk.
"It is smart of me to pay with my charge card."

"Yes," says the woman in back of her. "It can be smart to charge it.
But some cannot handle charge cards very well.
They charge many large bills.
They can pay for just part of their bills.
But they charge and charge until it gets hard for them to pay.
When they cannot pay, the store takes back their things.
Their charge cards have hurt them."

"Yes," Marge says. "You have to watch out when you charge things.
I am glad I can pay for what I charge.
Charge cards will never harm me.
I can handle them well."

Marge hurries out of the store with two large bags in her arms.
She thinks, "You have to be pretty smart just to shop in a department store!"

Appendix A: Helping Students Decode Words with Blends

Words with blends are often difficult for the student to decode. It is important that he have a good knowledge of consonant sounds and short vowel sounds before doing this book. If you discover he needs more help with these sounds as he starts this book, give him more practice with them before he works on decoding words with blends.

In the blends practices, words are always grouped together by similar beginning or ending blends. To introduce sounding out the blend, two words are used. For beginning blends, the first letter of the blend is added to the first word to make the second word (*rag/brag*). So the student discovers, for example, how the beginning blend /br/ differs from the single consonant sound /r/ in words. You may want to give him more examples and practice with word pairs like these. Or, if he still seems unsure of the sound of the blend, you may try contrasting the blend with the other consonant sounds in word pairs—by comparing *brag* with *bag*, for example. For most of the ending blends, the last letter of the blend is added to the first word to make the second word (*ban/band*). You may want to compare the blend with the other consonant sound (compare *band* with *bad,* for example). This kind of practice may help the student learn and recognize the blend sounds better.

If he has learned a beginning or ending blend sound well, he should consistently pronounce it correctly in the word lists. His next task is to "blend" the blend sound with other beginning or ending sounds and a short vowel sound in words. For some students, this may be a difficult and laborious process. Often you must let him try to blend the sounds in the way he can do it best, ignoring the practice dialog. A student working on the ending blend *-nd,* for example, may combine the *a* and *nd* into an ending stem /and/, and then try to blend beginning consonant sounds with /and/. Or he may blend the beginning sounds and the /a/ sound first, and then add the blend sounds /nd/ to the end. Or he may try to pronounce each sound individually, blending the sounds together into a word. You must explore with your student the methods of decoding which will work best.

If he knows and can pronounce the individual sounds in the word, but substitutes some different sounds when he blends them together, he may have a problem with auditory memory. He may have difficulty remembering the sounds, or remembering their order in a word. Another common decoding problem, especially with blend words, is reversing or changing the order of some sounds (*ruts* for *rust, trap* for *tarp,* or *stop* for *spot*). For all of these problems, you might help the student by writing down what he actually says. Then he can see how he has sounded out a word and can compare it with how it should be sounded out. This process can pinpoint troublesome sounds or parts of words, or can suggest different methods S. can use in decoding words.

Other students may have a lot of difficulty blending sounds together in general. You may want to have them practice blending sounds by giving them individual sounds, just a moment apart, to blend. If you do this, avoid attaching any vowel sounds to the individual consonant sounds. You may want to blend some sounds yourself, having the student repeat after you.

Finally, with some students you may want to avoid a phonetic approach altogether. These students find it easier to learn words as wholes. They have difficulty learning words by breaking them down and sounding them out, or by blending sounds together. For these students, you might want to try other techniques, such as kinesthetic tracing.

Foreign students and students with certain dialects may have special difficulties with blend words. For references outlining sounds foreign students may have trouble with, see *Pronunciation Contrasts in English* by Don L. F. Nilsen and Alleen Pace Nilsen (New York: Regents Publishing Company, Inc., 1973) and chapter 14, "Consonant Clusters," in *Manual of American English Pronunciation* by Clifford H. Prator, Jr. and Betty Wallace Robinett (New York: Holt, Rinehart and Winston, Inc., 1972). For an excellent analysis of Black English which includes a discussion of pronunciation features teachers should be aware of, see the chapter "Some Linguistic Features of Negro Dialect," by Ralph W. Fasold and Walt Wolfram, in *Black American English, Its Background and Its Usage in the Schools and in Literature,* edited by Paul Stoller (New York: Dell Publishing Co., 1975).

Appendix B: Creating Your Own Exercises for Word Endings

In *Skill Book 2* of Laubach Way to Reading and in *Focus on Phonics-2A: Short Vowel Sounds,* the student had practice with the endings *-s, -ing, -y,* and *-er.* There was more limited practice with endings *-es, -ies, -ied,* and *-ier.* There are no endings practices in this book, but you are encouraged to make up your own endings exercises for the endings you want your student to practice.

You may want to make exercises each time the student finishes a group of blends, using the blend words the student has just studied. (Blend words with *-y* and *-er* are in Appendixes C and D respectively, in the order the blends appear in this book.

This appendix can give you some ideas for exercises. In the sample exercises below, the *-s* ending is used on words that are both *nouns* and *verbs.* The *-er* ending can mean either "person or thing that does something," or "more." The endings *-ing, -ed, -er,* and *-y* are used on words in which the last consonant of the root word is doubled (words ending with Consonant-Vowel-Consonant) and where it is not doubled (words ending with Vowel-Consonant-Consonant). And the *-ing, -ed,* and *-er* endings are also used on words ending with *e*.

In your exercises, you may want to cover only certain endings, and certain types of words, for example, words in which the last consonant is doubled before adding the ending. Or, you may mix several endings or types of words together, depending on what your student should practice.

Often, students need many exercises to get enough practice with endings. Be sure your student knows the blend words that you plan to use in the exercise well.

Add the ending. Then read the word.

-s	step	________	*-er*	fast	________
-ing	print	________	*-y*	grab	________
-ing	take	________	*-es*	glass	________
-ed	test	________	*-ies*	baby	________
-er	farm	________	*-ier*	funny	________

Take off the ending. Write the root word.

belts	________	dancer	________
spinning	________	thicker	________
pressed	________	lumpy	________

Circle all the words that are the same as the first one.

spelled spells speller spelled spelling spelled speller

You may want to have students add endings to words that appear in sentences. You can make exercises in which the word appears before the sentence, and the student adds the ending and writes the word in the blank. Or you may want to put the root word below the blank in the sentence.

Add the ending. Fill in the blank. Read the sentence.

-s	clock	He sells ten ________ .
-ing	swim	Ed is ________ in the river.
-ing	rinse	Jan is ________ her hair.
-ed	slip	Bill ________ on the steps.
-ed	dance	She ________ with Tim.
-er	build	The ________ is working.
-er	write	Fred is a ________ .
-er	fresh	Your eggs are ________ .
-er	slim	That skirt is ________ .
-y	chill	It is ________ out there.
-y	edge	She felt a little ________ .
-es	glass	Rinse the ________ .
-es	brush	She ________ her hair.
-ies	city	He visits two ________ .
-ing	hurry	Jack is ________ .
-ied	carry	I ________ the box.
-ier	worry	Dad is a ________ .
-ier	pretty	Ann is ________ than Kim.

Appendix C: Words with *-y* Endings

In this Appendix and Appendix D, the words are grouped in the order in which their roots appear in the book. Sight words introduced in the practices are also listed. The groups are separated in this way to make it easier for the teacher to have the student practice the *-y* and *-er* endings after finishing each blend group.

Words in which the root word ends with *e* have an asterisk (*) in front of them. For these words, the *e* is dropped before the *-y* ending is added. If the student has not studied *-y* endings on words that end with *e*, you may want to point out these words.

The ending *-y* is often added to nouns or verbs to make adjectives. The ending *-y* can mean *full of, like, somewhat,* or *having* as in *dirty, crabby, chilly,* and *classy.*

Key to Grouping of Words

I. Review of Beginning and Ending Digraphs
II. Beginning Blends with *l*
III. Beginning Blends with *r*
IV. Beginning Blends with *s* and *w*
V. Beginning Three-letter Blends
VI. Review of Beginning Blends
VII. Ending Blends with *n*
VIII. Other Ending Blends
IX. Vowels + *r*

-*y* words in which last consonant of root word is *not* doubled:

I
chilly
catchy
patchy
itchy
fishy

II
blotchy
classy
flashy
fleshy
fluffy
plucky
glassy
slushy

III
brassy
cranky
dressy
frilly
grassy
trashy
tricky

IV
sticky
stinky
stocky
stuffy
smelly
*smudgy
sketchy

V
stretchy
stringy
scratchy
springy

VII
minty
handy
sandy
windy
crunchy
*chancy
springy
stringy
stinky
junky

VIII
bumpy
dumpy
lumpy
misty
dusty
gusty
musty
rusty
crusty
trusty
pesty
testy
risky
husky
crispy
guilty
milky
silky
crafty
drafty
shifty
thrifty

IX
jerky
perky
*nervy
whirly
squirmy
dirty
thirsty
curly
*curvy
hardy
marshy
starchy
corny
thorny
shorty
sporty
stormy
pearly
earthy
wordy
wormy
worthy

-*y* words in which last consonant of root word *is* doubled:

I
chatty
choppy

II
clammy
floppy

III
bratty
crabby
drippy
grabby
gritty
grubby

IV
spotty
snappy
snobby
smoggy
skinny

V
scrappy

IX
furry
blurry
starry

Appendix D: Words with *-er* Endings

Please read the first paragraph of Appendix C. It applies to this Appendix also.
Words with an asterisk (*) are those in which the root words end with an *e*, and only an *r* is added for the *-er* ending.

Agent Nouns: In these words, the *-er* usually means *a person or thing that does something.*

-*er* words in which last consonant of the root word is *not* doubled:

I

- shocker
- checker
- thinker
- whistler
- catcher
- pitcher
- dasher
- masher

II

- blinker
- blocker
- blusher
- flasher
- flicker

III

- cracker
- crasher
- crusher
- dresser
- drinker
- player
- trucker

IV

- sticker
- stringer
- stinker
- stuffer
- speller
- swinger

V

- stretcher
- scratcher
- thriller

VII

- planter
- renter
- printer
- hunter
- punter
- lender
- sender
- blender
- spender
- sander
- rancher
- quencher
- puncher
- *dancer
- *plunger
- hanger
- ringer
- singer
- stinger
- swinger
- banker
- tanker
- sinker
- thinker
- drinker
- stinker

VIII

- camper
- damper
- bumper
- jumper
- stumper
- twister
- duster
- tester
- husker
- crisper
- welder
- builder
- scalper
- helper
- golfer
- lifter
- sifter
- drifter

IX

- herder
- merger
- server
- twirler
- surfer
- curler
- turner
- burner
- marker
- charmer
- farmer
- gardener
- charter
- starter
- marcher
- *lover
- sorter
- scorcher
- *forger
- earner
- learner
- searcher
- worker

-*er* words in which last consonant of root word *is* doubled:

I

- shipper
- shopper
- shutter
- chatter
- chopper

II

- blotter
- clapper
- clipper
- flapper
- flipper
- planner
- slipper
- slugger

III

- dropper
- drummer
- trapper
- trimmer
- trotter

IV

- stopper
- spinner
- snapper
- scanner
- swimmer

V

- stripper
- scrubber
- shredder

Comparative Adjectives: In these words, the *-er* means *more.*

-*er* words in which last consonant of the root word is *not* doubled:

I

- thicker
- richer
- fresher

II

- blacker
- sticker

III

- drunker
- fresher

IV

- stiffer
- smarter

VII

- fonder

VIII

- damper
- faster
- crisper
- swifter
- stricter

IX

- firmer
- darker
- larger
- harder
- sharper
- smarter
- harsher
- newer
- shorter

-*er* words in which last consonant of root word *is* doubled:

I

- thinner

II

- flatter
- slimmer

Appendix E: Compound Words

All of the compound words in this list are made up of words that the student has learned in this series.

aftermath
anything
armpit
backdrop
backhand
backtrack
bandstand
barnyard
birdbath
birthday
birthmark
blackbird
blackjack
blacklist
blacksmith
blacktop
blockhead
breadbasket
buckskin
carport
chopstick
clockwork
cornstarch
crabgrass
crackdown
crackpot
dipstick
downcast
downwind
dropout
drumstick
dustpan
earthworm
eggplant
everything
farmhand
farmland
filmstrip
fingerprint
firstborn
firsthand
flashback
forklift
gangland
grandchildren
grandfather
grandmother
grandstand
grillwork
hairbrush
hamstring
handbag
handstand
hangman
hangover
hardback
hardcover
hardtop
headband
headdress
headfirst
herself
himself
horseback
humdrum
inchworm
inkblot
itself
kickstand
kingpin
landfill
landmark
leftover
lipstick
locksmith
lovebird
manhunt
markdown
milkman
myself
newscast
newsprint
newsstand
northwest
offhand
oneself
outburst
outcast
outlast
outrank
outsmart
outstanding
overspend
overstock
overstrict
overact
overcast
overdraft
overhand
overhang
overhead
overheard
overland
overturn
overwork
packhorse
passport
password
patchwork
pigskin
pinworm
pitchfork
plaything
popcorn
printout
quicksand
rattrap
redwing
ringworm
riverbank
sandbag
sandbar
sandblast
sandman
sandpaper
sandstorm
sharkskin
shipyard
shoplift
shopworn
shortcut
shorthand
shortstop
silkworm
skinflint
slingshot
snapshot
something
spendthrift
splashdown
sportscast
sportsman
sportswoman
standby
standoff
standstill
starfish
stepbrother
stepfather
stepmother
stepson
stinkbug
stockyard
stopgap
stopwatch
streetcar
sunburn
sunburst
sunglasses
sunlamp
sunspot
switchman
thanksgiving
turnabout
turnout
turnover
underarm
underbrush
undercover
underhand
underpants
undershirt
undershorts
understand
understudy
underworld
upbringing
upbuild
upland
uplift
upstanding
upstart
upswing
upturn
upwind
watchband
watchword
watercolor
watermark
wellspring
wetland
windbag
windburn
windchill
windmill
windstorm
windswept
wingspan
witchcraft
workbench
workday
workhorse
workman
yardstick
yourself

Appendix F: Words That End with CC-*le*

This list includes words from Practice 53A-B, plus some other words that you may wish to introduce to your student.

-bble
babble
dabble
pebble
dribble
nibble
scribble
gobble
wobble
bubble

-ddle
paddle
saddle
straddle
meddle
peddle
fiddle
griddle
middle
riddle
coddle
toddle
cuddle
huddle
muddle
puddle

-ffle
baffle
raffle
sniffle
muffle
ruffle
scuffle
shuffle

-ggle
giggle
jiggle
wiggle
juggle
smuggle
snuggle
struggle

-pple
apple
cripple
nipple
ripple
topple

-ssle
hassle
tussle

-ttle
battle
cattle
rattle
tattle
kettle
settle
brittle
little
whittle
bottle
throttle
shuttle

-zzle
dazzle
drizzle
fizzle
sizzle
nozzle
guzzle
muzzle
puzzle

-ckle
cackle
crackle
tackle
freckle
heckle
speckle
pickle
sickle
tickle
trickle
buckle
chuckle

-ndle
candle
handle
kindle
spindle
swindle
bundle

-ntle
gentle
mantle

-ncle
uncle

-ngle
angle
dangle
jangle
mangle
strangle
tangle
jingle
mingle
shingle
single
tingle
jungle

-nkle
ankle
crinkle
sprinkle
tinkle
twinkle

-mple
ample
sample
trample
temple
dimple
pimple
simple
crumple

-mble
gamble
ramble
scramble
tremble
thimble
bumble
crumble
fumble
grumble
humble
jumble
mumble
rumble
stumble
tumble

-stle
castle
nestle
bristle
gristle
thistle
whistle
bustle
hustle
rustle

r-C-le
marble
curdle
girdle
hurdle
sparkle
startle
circle
gargle
gurgle
purple
turtle